GUARDIANSHIPS AND THE ELDERLY
THE PERFECT CRIME

DR. SAM SUGAR

SQUAREONE
PUBLISHERS

Please note all material stories and accounts in this book are for general information only. The information in this book is not legal advice, should not be relied upon as legal or medical advice, may not be current, and is subject to change without notice.

In an effort to avoid awkward phrasing within sentences, it is our publishing style to alternate the use of male and female pronouns according to chapter. Therefore, when referring to a "third-person" adult, child, healthcare provider, or caregiver, odd-numbered chapters will use male pronouns, while even-numbered chapters will use female, to give acknowledgment to people of both genders.

Square One Publishers
115 Herricks Road
Garden City Park, NY 11040
(516) 535-2010 • (877) 900-BOOK
www.squareonepublishers.com

COVER DESIGNER: Jeannie Tudor
EDITOR: Allison Cirruzzo
TYPESETTER: Gary A. Rosenberg

Quote on pages 79-80 appears courtesy of Kenneth Ditkowsky.
Quote on pages 195-196 appears courtesy of Juan C. Antúnez, Esq.

Library of Congress Cataloging-in-Publication Data
Names: Sugar, Sam, Dr., author.
Title: Guardianship and the elderly : the perfect crime / Dr. Sam Sugar.
Description: Garden City Park, NY : Square One Publishers, [2018] | Includes
   bibliographical references and index.
Identifiers: LCCN 2018012112 (print) | LCCN 2018008389 (ebook) | ISBN
   9780757004339 (pbk. : alk. paper) | ISBN 9780757054334 (paperback)
Subjects: LCSH: Guardian and ward—United States. | Guardian and ward—United
   States—Criminal provisions. | Older people—Legal status, laws,
   etc.—United States. | Older people—Abuse of—United States. | Capacity
   and disability—United States.
Classification: LCC KF553 .S84 2018 (ebook) | LCC KF553 (print) | DDC
   346.7301/8—dc23
LC record available at HYPERLINK "https://lccn.loc.gov/2018012112" https://
lccn.loc.gov/2018012112

Printed in the United States of America

10   9   8   7   6   5   4   3   2

Contents

Part 3. Fighting the System

Acknowledgments

Exposing a monolithic scheme that exploits people just like you can be a very lonely undertaking. Writing a book like this is also a very personal experience. In my case, I was able to draw on the people and incredible stories I've been dealing with in my role as founder of Americans Against Abusive Probate Guardianship (AAAPG), as well as the advice of my parents. My experience in the practice of internal medicine for over forty-five years was instrumental in helping me understand the fallout, both physical and emotional, of being involved in this egregious "industry" of elder abuse.

My parents survived the Holocaust, making me a second-generation Holocaust survivor—an identity that I have only recently begun to embrace, but one that surely influenced my determination to expose this governmental scheme that destroys people and families. My parents taught me the nobility of fighting against all odds to survive. They insisted that their children—myself and my two brothers, David and Michael—always comport themselves with integrity. Although my parents were not the beneficiaries of higher education, their strength of will and purpose made them seem far more noble to me than any of my very highly educated circle of friends and colleagues.

I became passionate about this subject and decided to write this book after having been exposed to the guardianship process through the experiences of a loved one. I witnessed how overwhelming the guardianship process can be and how seemingly impossible it is to prevent or stop. This ordeal introduced me to outrages that I have since seen repeated countless times in the American professional guardianship industry.

I hope that through this book those suffering as a result of guardianship will derive some solace, and that this scheme will now become something other than a secret weapon unleashed on so many individuals and families.

Early on, I developed a relationship with the late Latifa Ring, whose own personal experience with guardianship ultimately killed her with what I believe was a stress-induced malignancy. She was one of the first people to recognize the evil nature of guardianship and fought with every ounce of her being against it.

Attorney Ken Ditkowsky, from my hometown of Chicago, is another advocate who continues to expose the evil that is abusive guardianship. His vast experience in the law has been of great assistance to me in understanding the nuts and bolts of what guardianship should be, as well as what it actually is.

I met Lidya Abaramovici by accident and found that we had both suffered from the slings and arrows of guardianship. We developed a wonderful working relationship. Without her, none of the accomplishments of our group would have been possible. She is a dynamo and a true warrior for justice.

Another warrior is Doug Franks, who spent every waking moment of his life fighting for the freedom of his mother, Ernestine, until her passing, and even since then. He endured threats of incarceration and enormous monetary sacrifice to let the world know what guardianship did to his mother and family. Driving around all of Florida with his "Free Ernestine" banner prominently displayed on his car probably brought more attention to this cause than anything else.

Lynn and Alan Sayler have been unwavering supporters of our work. They are committed to seeing justice done for victims like Lynn's mother, who died in guardianship.

Attorney Greg Coleman, former president of the Florida Bar Association and a member of the Judicial Qualifications Committee, has been generous with his time and advice since the week he became president of the bar. He showed compassion and understanding of the issue and has always been a friend and a resource to me.

John Pacenti, an extraordinary investigative reporter in Palm Beach, Florida, called me at the very beginning of my journey in guardianship and wanted a story from me about the subject. At the time, I was so terrified that I refused to speak to him or give him my full contact information. He persisted and, some time later, he and I began a collaboration that has spanned half a decade and resulted in the most striking exposés of the abject corruption in Palm Beach Circuit Court. John is a brave and courageous man who stands up for the truth and for people who have been so badly injured by the court corruption he writes about. I am honored to call him my friend.

Attorney Michael Schlesinger of Miami, Florida, has allowed me to retain a little faith in the legal profession. He has done his best to help my family and the countless others who have been referred to him. His candor, professionalism, and diligence were exactly what we needed in a time of desperate legal peril, from which he helped us escape with his expertise in our appeal to the third District Court of Appeal in Miami.

From the time I met her near Orlando, Florida, where we filmed our documentary *Broken*, Kelley Smoot Garrett has been a brave, wonderful, and dedicated colleague. Her energy, skill, and dedication are endless. Without her and her expertise in IT, our message would have reached far fewer people.

A very special thank you to my great friend Jon Huntsman Sr., whose generosity and faith in me allowed for the creation of AAAPG and all it has accomplished.

I want to thank Ally Cirruzzo and Michael Weatherhead, my editors, as well as Anthony Pomes, at Square One Publishers, for their tireless work on this project. Their patience and skills were the glue that held it all together.

The victims of abusive guardianship who call us for help deserve recognition as well. I hope that over time, the number of victims, the number of guardianships, and the number of horrific stories will decrease.

My wife Judy is a special woman. Her strength of character and love for me sustained me in times of trouble. Her courage and wisdom in the face of adversity has sustained me and given me hope. Without her love and support this book could never have been written. I love and treasure you, Judy. This book is in honor of you and in loving memory of Chayele.

Sam Sugar, MD
Hollywood, Florida

Foreword

There is a powerful guardianship industry in the United States, but, for the most part, its power is unknown and unchallenged. Dr. Sam Sugar, more than anyone else in our country, is expanding public awareness that the industry is broken and needs to change.

Our country's history is full of calls to increase our civic awareness. President Dwight Eisenhower warned us about a dire threat to democratic government known as the military-industrial complex. Rachel Carson's Silent Spring, published in the summer of 1962, informed us of the adverse effects of pesticide use on our environment. Martin Luther King Jr.'s "I Have a Dream" speech deeply affected us and called us to live up to the principles this country is said to espouse. It is the hope of many—including myself—that *Guardianships and the Elderly* will prove to be a similar catalyst for change.

Unchecked power is frequently overlooked or undetected. As a result, the deprivation of rights often goes unacknowledged until it is spotlighted or directly experienced. Lutheran pastor Martin Niemöller's quotation on display in the permanent exhibition of the United States Holocaust Memorial Museum both exemplifies the human tendency to avoid confrontation as well as the evil of silence in the face of injustice:

> First they came for the Socialists, and I did not speak out—
> Because I was not a Socialist.

Then they came for the Trade Unionists, and I did not speak out—
Because I was not a Trade Unionist.

Then they came for the Jews, and I did not speak out—
Because I was not a Jew.

Then they came for me—
and there was no one left to speak for me.

It takes courage, commitment, and sacrifice to speak out. Deep-seated institutional power coupled with the veil of secrecy make guardianship industry abusers potent foes, and those who challenge such abuse generally find few allies. Nevertheless, widening public awareness is a key ingredient to facilitating positive developments. This book, both an indictment of a troubled system as well as a principled call to action, is a terrific resource for families, media outlets, and legislators who wish to fight for a better way. It is a powerful resource that exposes a structure in need of being remade. Dr. Sugar is the founder of Americans Against Abusive Probate Guardianship (AAAPG) and a recognized national voice in challenging the widespread abusive practices of those who are supposed to protect our seniors.

Moral necessity and demographic shifts demand reform. The United States has some 75 million baby boomers, 10,000 of which reach the age of 65 every day. The boomer generation, greatly invested in social change since its youth, can now be a powerful source of change in its advancing age. Calls for new laws to protect seniors against guardianship abuse combined with growing awareness make the baby boomer generation natural allies of those calling for significant changes to the guardianship industry.

It has been my pleasure in life to know people who, sometimes at great personal cost, make a difference in the lives of others. Dr. Sugar is surely one of those people. My personal heroes are always people like Dr. Sugar: courageous, committed, and clearly focused on making things better for other people.

Identifying the spark that sets off such commitment is not always easy. In Dr. Sugar we are given some strong hints. He is a second-generation Holocaust survivor, a child of parents who taught him the nobility of fighting against all odds to survive. I've seen such nobility before, in those who deserve our society's highest regard but for whom this regard has not yet been granted: a granddaughter of an American slave, a person with overwhelming physical disabilities whose greatest concern is for those around him, and a chronic Good Samaritan whose life was ended by a drunk driver. It is vital to remember people who sacrifice for others, those who fight against what seem like unsurmountable odds.

I first met Dr. Sugar when he contacted me about my book, *The Wolf at the Door: Undue Influence and Elder Financial Abuse.* We talked about the book and how it represented my own effort to make a difference in the way our society approaches the protection of elders from financial abuse. Through our conversations, I learned more about him and his national leadership in shining a light on the personal and familial suffering occasioned by guardianship abuse. Abusive guardians unchecked are well past the elder's door—they are in the house.

I've been a lawyer for over forty years. Given my professional background, I was drawn to the observations about lawyers and guardianship cases Dr. Sugar makes in this book. After noting that guardianships are fueled by family disputes, he writes that "litigators representing all sides can take full advantage of these situations and may even intentionally stoke the flames of discord, all for the one thing that drives them: legal fees." I've seen this up close, unfortunately. Not all guardianship cases involve this kind of misconduct, but when one does it is disquieting and disgusting, and amounts to a blight on my profession. It feels dirty to sit at a table with lawyers who seem to have forgotten the people they are supposed to serve. Professionals charge fees; this is an economic reality. But neglecting the needs of clients and gouging them with exorbitant fees should not be a reality. I credit Dr. Sugar for identifying this very serious problem.

I think that Dr. Sugar's book will profoundly influence people's lives. The more attention this book receives, the more lives will benefit. I don't say this to add dramatic flourish; it is the simple truth. There is great meaning in this book. It is a clarion call to our better selves—those selves who will speak and act against abusive power.

–Michael Hackard, Esq.
Author of *The Wolf at the Door*

Preface

I wish I had never heard the term "guardianship." I wish the facts and stories I am about to share had never happened. But as Albert Einstein said, "Those who have the privilege to know, have the duty to act." Thousands of unsuspecting, well-meaning Americans have experienced life-altering abuse at the hands of a little-known and poorly understood court-based system known as professional guardianship. The kinds of injustice, expense, and despair that I have personally witnessed in Florida's probate court system—where thousands of guardianships are handed out every year—continue to be experienced by so many families across this nation.

Initially, we thought our experience must be a one-of-a-kind horror show that was just our bad luck, an unfortunate series of circumstances, an exception to what we believed to be an honest and just court system. But over time, as we came across more and more victims of professional guardianship abuse throughout our home state of Florida, and then throughout the country, we realized this unfathomably horrible process was all too common.

At a certain point, I knew something needed to be done to draw attention to what was going on, so in 2012, I decided to take matters into my own hands. I formed Americans Against Abusive Probate Guardianship (AAAPG) with the goal to "educate, advocate, and legislate" for families caught up in probate exploitation. The organization's goal is to raise awareness of the threat of abusive guardianship and fight to eliminate these abuses.

Gradually, as I was exposed to dozens and then hundreds of cases of guardianship abuse as founder of AAAPG, a recurrent pattern of events emerged that shocked me. It seemed that judges, guardians, and lawyers in courts across the country had developed a systematic playbook to be used in generating and perpetuating immensely lucrative, professional guardianships. These professionals essentially guaranteed guardianship industry insiders easy and total access to the lives and assets of unsuspecting individuals who potentially needed help managing their affairs or their health because of something called their "incapacity"—their putative inability to function safely on their own.

I slowly learned that there is something terribly wrong with the American guardianship system. The imposition of court-imposed involuntary professional guardianship is all too often merely a devious, slick ploy—an arcane, poorly understood legalistic court process that perverts existing laws meant to protect the vulnerable into an exploitative system.

The more time I spent studying this issue, the angrier I got. I simply could not believe that there was a system in place in this country that could strip innocent individuals of their constitutional rights, seize their assets without due process, and relegate them to living the rest of their days under the total control of other people. Even worse, often these guardians know nothing about their court-appointed wards but have unfettered control over their savings, property, healthcare, and virtually every other aspect of their lives. I simply could not understand how any component of our legal system could possibly turn a blind eye to such cruelty. I (and many others) wondered how it could be happening in the United States.

What I learned is that it happens all the time. This nationwide system of abuse is rapidly expanding, posing a stealthy but very real threat to older Americans and their families.

Here are some things I discovered:

● There are millions of individuals in this situation in America.

● The statistics on guardianship that would allow legitimate study of the issue are intentionally kept hidden from the public.

- Legitimate complaints about guardianship have fallen on deaf ears at every level of our government for over forty years and continue to fall on deaf ears in state capitals and Washington, DC.

- The normal sets of checks and balances that our government depends on to retain its legitimacy simply do not exist in guardianship "equity" courts.

On my personal journey, I have met and befriended important leaders in the legal, judicial, and legislative communities who are convinced that reform is urgently needed. But I have also come across very powerful groups in these same communities that are determined to prevent reform and keep their industry flying under the radar at any cost. This system, which long ago may have been set up to protect the most vulnerable people in our society, is now a massive, well-organized, for-profit business. Court insiders will always fight tooth and nail to protect their turf, their power, and their easy access to your family's money. Along my journey I have also encountered many hundreds of fine people, honest people, loving sons, loving daughters, and relatives of victims, all of whom have suffered enormously as a result of the guardianship system. The stories they have shared with me are all similar tales of physical, financial, and mental torment.

I hope this book sheds sufficient light on this system run amok, which has allowed guardianship courts to be controlled by the very people who profit from their protected positions. I also hope it teaches you some important tips that might help you avoid this process, shield your loved ones and yourself from its painful results, or pursue legislative changes to the guardianship system in your area and across the country.

Introduction

"We used to fear getting cancer,
now we fear guardianship even more."
—FAMILY MEMBERS OF A VICTIM OF GUARDIANSHIP

We all pray for long life in hopes that our golden years will be spent in comfort, harmony, and peace, and that the assets, money, and property we have accumulated over our lifetimes will be distributed to or inherited by our loved ones as we wish and see fit. But in America, no matter how well you have planned, no matter how painstakingly your estate plan has been created, no matter how much you have or do not have, there lurks a serious, shadowy threat to every elderly citizen's well-being and the execution of their end-of-life wishes.

Worse, it is a threat that is rapidly growing throughout the country and leaving in its wake plundered estates, broken families, and the shattered lives of those who have been deemed "incapacitated." This threat is called *professional guardianship*, and unfortunately, the quote above aptly represents the feelings of many of those who have experienced this all too powerful court-based process.

There is a good chance that the average American has never heard of the legal process involved in imposing and carrying out guardianships. It is also likely that you equate the term "guardian" with the word "protector." And as a legal process, without a clear understanding of what a guardianship actually entails, it would likely conjure up something designed to help people in need—a process in which a court is able to see after the welfare of an individual. However, once a family becomes embroiled in the actual process of a professional guardianship, a true picture emerges of a process that would, in any other circumstance, be deemed illegal and certainly unconstitutional.

While there are various types of legal guardianships, the ones we will focus on in the coming chapters are professional, for-profit guardianships (also known as conservatorships and simply referred to in this book as "guardianships") in which a court hands over absolute control of the life of a person who has been procedurally and legally deemed incapable of adequately taking care of him or herself—and who has assets. These assets can include homes, savings and brokerage accounts, jewelry, and social security payments, as well as any property of value.

The judges and courts that manage and implement this system as part of the judiciary in every state are governed by statutes and special court rules unique to each one. These rules, regulations, and standards are interpreted and administered under the direction of a specific kind of court and, in many cases, by specific judges. Generally, it is the state probate court that deals with adult guardianships.

Although probate courts may be referred to by different names from state to state, their tasks remain essentially the same. These tasks include responding to and establishing the need for a guardianship to be put into place; selecting the guardian or guardians to oversee and manage the ward's finances, living conditions, and healthcare; monitoring and/or setting fees and living expenses taken from the ward's assets; monitoring the guardian's duties and obligations; and ending the guardianship expediently based upon a legal proceeding or upon the death of the ward.

On the face of it, a guardianship sounds reasonable. A ward, whom the courts deem as unable to take care of herself under this system, can be looked after through the care and guidance of a court-appointed professional guardian. Any costs involved would be paid for by simply withdrawing funds from the ward's assets under the watchful eyes of the court administrators. The ward would be safe and protected from exploitation, abuse, and neglect, and her family relieved from the work of caring for an elderly person, all under the watchful supervision of a benevolent judge. Sounds good!

Unfortunately, over the years, all across the country, the guardianship process has not only broken down, but has morphed into a dangerous system working above the law and in violation of the basic freedoms granted to each of us under the Constitution of the United States. It is yet another example of the veracity of the old adage, "absolute power corrupts absolutely."

As you will see, these professional guardianships have become immensely profitable sources of income, not only for the guardians and the people they hire, but also for the lawyers and judges who oversee the process. The profit motive that now drives the professional guardianship system relegates actually providing care and support for an elderly person to a minor, trivial matter. So often, wards' basic needs are of little concern to the busy guardian.

Many wards are routinely handed off to inexperienced low-level caregivers, whom they depend on for their very existence. Amazingly, the ward's family, who no longer have any control over her life, can only watch to see what living facility or nursing home she is placed in, who her doctors are, or which medications she is prescribed. Even if the ward has legally set forth her wishes for end-of-life care and inheritance distribution prior to the establishment of the guardianship, those documents are no longer enforceable under the rules of guardianship. For the families, it is a terrifying and helpless feeling—multiplied a thousand-fold for the helpless piece of property known as the ward.

It may not seem like this could happen in the United States, but it goes on every day through the guardianship programs in place throughout the country. So why have you not heard of these abuses? The fact that you have not may very well be by design. The system is quite content to fly under the radar. And yes, every once in a while, you will read about a guardian who is convicted for embezzling very large amounts of money, like:

- Patience Bristol of Las Vegas, Nevada, a former professional guardian who is now in prison after pleading guilty to exploitation of a vulnerable person. She "tapped the accounts of her [four] wards to cover her sizable gambling debts and personal expenses," totaling $495,000 in just one case.

- April Parks, also of Las Vegas, a professional guardian whose criminal sentence is pending after an $8.5 million-dollar civil judgment.

- Paul Donisthorpe of New Mexico, who was convicted after stealing millions of dollars from the elderly and disabled through his trust company, Desert State Life Management. He was sentenced to eight to twelve years in prison and must pay over $4 million in restitution to the victims of his crimes.

But even that is only a blip in an endlessly large ocean of cash that court insiders extract every year with no fear. They know how to play the system, and lawyers especially are not very worried about being prosecuted because they are "legally" working within a system ripe for abuse. A judge's signature makes everything and anything they do "legal."

On the other hand, if you are familiar with the injustices of guardianship, you and your family may already be one of the thousands of people entangled in this unfair system. And the likelihood of being involved in a guardianship is increasing daily. Ten thousand baby boomers a day are turning sixty-five years of age. Projections based on demographics alone predict an enormous increase in the number of individuals with dementia or other forms of incapacity who will be trapped in involuntary guardianship over the next five to ten years. As many as one million new American wards have been created in the last decade alone.

I am a guardianship family survivor, a board-certified special-ist in Internal Medicine, an advocate for the elderly, and a certified guardianship examining committee member. I have witnessed firsthand and studied in depth the many glaring flaws in the way allegedly incapacitated individuals are treated in this bewildering court-based system of intrusion into the personal lives of innocent citizens.

As founder of Americans Against Abusive Probate Guardian-ship, I have had the opportunity to attain an in-depth insider's knowledge that, through the countless personal stories of our sub-scribers, paints a terribly disturbing picture of American guard-ianship so vividly. By telling those stories and the lessons learned from them, the average citizen can better understand what is, by design, an incomprehensible system so powerful as to rule over life and death.

Guardianships and the Elderly is the result of the combined efforts of myself and my dedicated colleagues to make this information public and accessible.

WHAT'S IN THIS BOOK

The information you will find in this book is designed to provide a clear picture of how this system works and how it does not. You will be introduced to two very different perspectives of mod-ern-day guardianship in the United States.

First, to understand guardianship and how it has evolved, you will learn details about what guardianship statutes were intended to accomplish—the way the system is supposed to work. But from a second, very real life perspective, you will learn how this complex and sometimes brutal system actually *does* work. The discrepancies between these two perspectives are glaring.

We will examine the critical differences between the types of courts that function as courts of *equity*, rather than courts of *law*. This critical distinction is what allows probate courts to function without juries and without any oversight or discipline. These courts and the judges who rule them are fully responsible for monitoring and disciplining guardians they appoint, but as you will see, there are innumerable conflicts of interest that impede the ability of the court to perform its work properly.

Next, we will explore the reality that guardians across the country are not licensed or meaningfully supervised in any way, and more importantly, often have little or no formal training, education, or background in the complex task of taking total responsibility for the life of the ward assigned to them. We will examine the guardian's roles and see how they are trained, supervised, and disciplined.

Then we will delve into the world of guardianship attorneys and understand how their connections to guardians and judges allow them to reap rewards for the mountains of paperwork they create, which do far more to protect the guardians than the innocent, vulnerable individuals. We will analyze the guardianship industry court insiders and their numerous downstream stakeholders, and why they are able to so greatly profit from the assets of wards.

You will learn what happens when anyone, including family members and even lawyers with years of experience, attempts to protest against seizure of civil rights and assets by the judges in charge. You will also discover some of the most common traps in the legal maze that disadvantage the uninitiated.

Finally, I will present critical tips to prevent abusive guardianships and suggestions for how to effectively rescue a ward trapped in one.

And much more.

This information is critical to every member of your family—because this guardianship catastrophe could easily happen to you. I offer this book to shed light on this powerful industry, so that potential wards and their loved ones can be better educated and prepared to protect their loved ones and even prevent an unnecessary guardianship from ever taking place.

So let's begin to understand how this all came to be.

PART 1

The Basics

1

What Is Guardianship?

"The administration of government, like a guardianship, ought to be directed to the good of those who confer, not of those who receive the trust."
—Marcus Tullius Cicero, Roman statesman
(106 BC to 43 BC)

If you walk through most towns or cities, chances are you will encounter homeless people on the streets, begging for food or money or both. Beyond living in poverty, many of these people suffer from physical, mental, or emotional disorders. Despite massive programs like Medicare, Medicaid, and worker's compensation, as a country, the United States does not have a cohesive national policy towards the care of these individuals. Instead, it is left to state and local governments, non-profits, and other groups to deal with the homeless community. There is little reward for the efforts of these organizations, except in the knowledge that they are helping poor souls in need of assistance.

On the other hand, in each state there exist court-administered rules, statutes, and programs that have been legally designed to step in and take over the care and lives of adult individuals who have assets but may not be able to take care of themselves. And unlike the many underfunded agencies that attempt to help the poor and vulnerable among us, this governmental system has turned the unfortunates who fall prey to it into a source of incredible riches for *court insiders*—that is, those individuals who benefit directly or indirectly from these court proceedings, and who do all they can to keep it quietly in place.

The system is called *professional guardianship.* This chapter looks at the history of guardianships and explores how they developed in the United States. As you will see, guardianship has been around for a very long time, and the methods employed in upholding this institution tend to reflect the society in which it exists. It should, therefore, not come as a surprise that the system of guardianship in a capitalist society such as the United States has become a highly profitable business. This chapter also explores both the public's perception of guardianship and its brutal reality.

A BRIEF HISTORY OF GUARDIANSHIP

The concept of guardianship—that is, one individual being responsible for another—can be traced back to the laws of ancient Athens in Greece (500 to 336 BC). The laws of that time primarily dealt with inheritance and the control of property and individuals. It was the Roman Republic (509 to 29 BC) that established the underlying principles of *parens patriae,* the concept that the state had the power to intervene in cases of child abuse and render help to incapacitated or disabled adults.

In 449 BC, the Centuriate Assembly in Rome ratified what would become known as the Law of the Twelve Tables. Among this set of laws, the rules of "Inheritance and Guardianships" were laid out. While it covered guardianships of children and women, it also covered guardianship of adults who could not care for themselves, specifically the insane:

> If a person is insane, authority over him and his personal property shall belong to his male agnates and in default of these to his male clansmen . . . but if there is not a guardian for him . . . Administration of his own goods shall be forbidden to a spendthrift

[a person who spends money in an irresponsible way]. . . . A spendthrift, who is forbidden from administering his own goods, shall be . . . under guardianship of his male agnates [paternal relative].

A paternal relative could be deemed a "guardian" in order to protect a person and his goods if that person were unable to take care of himself. It was under the Roman Empire (44 BC to 476 AD) that practice of government intervention was instituted under the principles of *parens patriae*. The position of guardian became a public office that was compulsory for all who qualified. Laws were put into place to protect children, adults, and the belongings of these individuals, from being abused by a guardian. When the Roman Empire fell, many of these rules were adopted by the Byzantine Empire, also called the Eastern Roman Empire (324 to 1453 AD).

During the Middle Ages (1300 to 1600 AD), European guardianships, while drawing upon Roman law, were greatly influenced by the feudal system and the church, which focused on children, property, military service, and inheritance. In England, common law set in place numerous guidelines for guardians overseeing minors through the royal and ecclesiastical courts. Early on, the English monarch took control of the property and assets of people with means who had been deemed "lunatics" or had intellectual disabilities in an effort to stop local feudal lords from taking advantage of these vulnerable parties first.

To manage and increase royal revenues and further maintain control over the possessions of his populace, Edward I of England enacted the Statutes of Mortmain in 1279 and 1290. (Possession of property by an institution such as the Church was known as "mortmain," which literally means "dead hand.") These statutes were aimed at preventing land from passing into the possession of the Church. They were created under the doctrine of *De Praerogativa Regis*, "the Royal Prerogative." Over time, this process was placed in the hands of the Church-run Court of Chancery (circa 1280 to 1852 AD). Initially operating under the *Curia Regis*, "the King's

Court," in 1345 AD, the Court of Chancery began to function separately, allowing it to make guardianship decisions independently.

From a legal point of view, the Court of Chancery operated as a *court of equity,* as opposed to a *court of law.* Whereas common law courts were required to adhere to the strict royal laws of the times, a court of equity could base its decisions on what it deemed "fair." The Court of Chancery was allowed to make legal decisions that could overrule or ignore common laws followed by other courts. It dealt with a wide variety of legal issues, including the guardianship of both children and adults. Unfortunately, those individuals with no family or property, or who were unable to care for themselves, were often ignored, isolated, or imprisoned.

During the 1800s, with the development of the British medical establishment, adults could be evaluated to see if their decision-making abilities were impaired. Under this approach, British mental health laws gave medical experts the power to decide whether individuals were legally "insane." Once found "insane," they could then be detained "for their own good" or for the safety of the community. This approach was used in the United Kingdom through much of the 1900s.

GUARDIANSHIP IN AMERICA

In America, the original thirteen colonies observed the English doctrine of "the King's Court" when dealing with well-to-do colonists. This doctrine was expanded to include the personal care of the incompetent adult as well. Unfortunately, the colonist with no assets or property could meet the same fate as his English counterpart—becoming ostracized or imprisoned. As a young, independent nation very concerned about states' rights, the responsibility of adult guardianship was placed squarely in the hands of each newly formed state's own government. Legislators would establish laws and guidelines to regulate and finance guardianships, and state judicial systems would carry out the process. Because adult guardianship proceedings included the oversight of property and assets, most states assigned these procedures to their *probate courts*—courts specifically in charge of cases dealing with wills and estates of the dead. While still legally considered "courts of law," these probate courts functioned as though they were "courts of equity," which, to this day, allows them to operate without juries or adherence to due process. For many years, probate courts were in charge of all matters involving interstate slave trade and directly responsible for the cruelty and abuse of that atrocity.

For almost two centuries, each state's adult guardianship system became subject to the self-interests and greed of the legislators making the laws and the judges making the decisions. While occasionally the financial or physical abuse of a ward was so horrendous that it made local headlines, the clear majority of people involved in these systems had learned to operate with impunity. With very little oversight from any quarter and the ability to keep an extremely low profile by not allowing court proceedings to be made public, guardianship systems allowed millions of wards to be taken advantage of by courts, guardians, and associates of both groups.

It was not until September 1987, after a year-long investigation by the *Associated Press*, that these stories of abuse were reported in a six-part series. Entitled "Guardians of the Elderly: An Ailing System," the series described these wards as "legally dead." After reviewing more than 2,200 guardianship files representing all fifty states, the reporters concluded that these systems were failing the very people they were designed to protect. Countless similar studies and exposés have followed, all revealing the ugly underside of this system.

The *Associated Press* series helped spur on a hearing by the United States House Committee on Aging, which was followed by a 1988 National Guardianship Symposium sponsored by the ABA Commission on Law and Aging and Commission on Mental and Physical Disability Law. Held in the Wingspread Conference Center in Wisconsin, the group issued thirty-one recommendations for improvements of the various systems. Known as the Wingspan

Conference, follow-up sessions were held in 2001, 2004, and 2011. In 2002, the following recommendation was made:

> Professional guardians—those who receive fees for serving two or more unrelated wards—should be licensed, certified, or registered. They should have the skills necessary to serve their wards. Professional guardians should be guided by professional standards and codes of ethics, such as the National Guardianship Association's *A Model Code of Ethics for Guardians and Standards of Practice.*

While the need for these fundamental measures remains unmet, over the years more recommendations have been presented and incorporated under a number of state laws. Unfortunately, while these new laws may have led to better statutes, guardianship courts have the ability to act as though they were "courts of equity," circumventing their own state laws.

More recently, the Elder Protection and Prosecution Act was passed and signed into law by President Donald Trump. This act mandated the first intervention by the federal government into elder and probate abuse with the activation of a national network to investigate and gather data on the incidence and prevalence of these wrongdoings. Yet, despite regular mainstream news stories of rampant abuse, corruption, exploitation, and constitutional violations, these guardianship systems continue to flourish and grow seemingly unabated throughout America.

SYSTEMS OF GUARDIANSHIP

Every state has probate-like equity courts to deal with money matters. These courts are charged with distributing assets of the deceased. In most states, probate courts also serve an additional function of protecting the lives and assets of individuals who cannot do so themselves. These people have committed no crime but have allegedly become, for whatever reason, "incapacitated." In other words, they have been judged incapable of caring for themselves. From state to state, court names may change, some laws and legal terminology may differ, and the process of carrying out specific tasks of care may vary, but the overall principles and tasks of these courts are similar enough to provide an accurate general picture of the system as a whole. (To view guardianship laws by state, consult the "In Your State" tab on the National Resource Center for Supported Decision-Making's website, www.supporteddecisionmaking.org.)

In most states, there are essentially two primary systems of guardianship, which are based on the wealth of the individual being placed under the system. One is designed for those with few meaningful financial resources. The other has been set up to oversee those who have financial assets.

Guardianship for Those with Few Assets

Public guardianships occur when indigent, or disadvantaged, individuals are identified by the court as in need of government assistance to allow them to be housed, fed, and maintained safely. As such, they are considered "wards of the state." Programs designed to support these individuals are often run by contractors hired by the state and funded through donations, state subsidies, grants, and federal programs. The process used to determine incapacity in indigent individuals is identical to the one used in connection with those who are not indigent, but the similarity ends there.

Public wards typically have no family member available or willing to assist them. With their assets being minimal, there is little to litigate over. Some states, including New York, do not provide public guardianships. Instead they use non-profits to provide various forms of assistance to needy, incapacitated individuals. But even these programs, which may be well intended, have been known to succumb to the lure of money.

Guardianship for Those with Assets

It is a different story for individuals with more wealth. Individuals with at least some assets, such as cash, real estate, a stock portfolio, pensions or legal settlements, may be placed into *family guardianships*—the most common type of guardianship—in which family members are appointed guardians, sometimes under the supervision of other court-appointed guardians. In other circumstances, a family member will be assigned an independent co-guardian, who will report back to the court. Under these systems, all court costs, guardian fees, and ancillary bills are paid using funds from the financial holdings of the ward, but managed by the family guardian. (This aspect is discussed in greater detail in Part 2.)

If no family is available or deemed appropriate by the court, wards may be taken into private, for-profit *professional guardianships* in which they are assigned by the court to approved state-certified professional guardians, who do this work for a living and are chosen from a supposedly rotating roster of court-approved guardians. These individuals are unilaterally selected by the court to act as substitute decision-makers for individuals who have assets. In some states, a ward may be assigned to a lawyer who has passed a simple guardianship test to become eligible as a court-approved guardian known as a guardian *ad litem*, whose duties include reporting status to the court.

SO, WHAT'S THE PROBLEM?

There is no question that there are many good and devoted individuals who work very hard on behalf of their wards and receive only meager compensation, but professional guardianship is all about money. In most public guardianships, which involve little litigation, there are minimal legal and guardianship fees, and limited opportunity for guardians and lawyers to improperly profit. This is not to say that public guardianships cannot generate serious money. Significant money can be made by court insiders who know how to play the public system—if not directly from their wards, then from the many governmental or charitable services designed to help the indigent. Based on what drives these guardians, it seems that you can get blood from a stone—or make money dealing with the very poorest of us. This book's focus, however, is the guardianship system that handles wards that have assets—a system of which few of us are aware until we find ourselves or someone we know caught in its web.

Perception Is Everything

When we hear the word "guardian," it conjures up images of superheroes, champions, or protectors. It may evoke images of nice people taking care of innocent children. One thing it does not do is set off alarm bells. Thanks, in part, to these reasons, this unfair system has been allowed to go unchecked for decades. Mainly, however, the subject of professional guardianship of adults with assets remains under the public's radar because it is being deliberately kept a secret by the countless court insiders who profit from the current system. It represents a sizable and steady income for a great number of people who do not want it publicized for fear of losing a cash cow.

Yes, every once in a while a really greedy guardian is caught taking hundreds of thousands or even millions of dollars from a ward's estate and the story makes headlines. Occasionally, meetings of well-meaning lawyers and government representatives who find themselves under pressure to come up with new guidelines for guardianship systems take place, sometimes leading to updated laws. Unfortunately, when this attention dies down, which it always does, court insiders go on quietly with their court-appointed guardianships unchanged, either ignoring new regulations or figuring out ways around them.

Then there is the ability of the court to sequester—or keep secret—the full guardianship records from ever being seen. Of course, the rationale for this power is based ostensibly on the court's need to maintain the privacy of the ward's estate. By sequestering records, however, the court also manages to keep any court insider's transactions just as private.

This is not to say that a ward's relatives or friends cannot lodge complaints against a judge or guardian. Each state has a formal group of legal professionals that is tasked with overseeing their colleagues and taking public complaints. Interested parties can send letters, documents, or detailed evidence of what is happening to a particular abused or exploited ward in the hope that something will be done to rectify the situation. Yet, for all the time and expense involved in filing a complaint, what normally happens—after a long waiting period—is dismissal of the complaint by the appropriate committee or the submission of a letter to the offending party, which essentially amounts to a light slap on the wrist. All the while, the estates of one ward after another are systematically depleted with no intervention or redress. This is the perverse "protection" offered by the very courts that, in theory, are supposed to look after wards and not their guardians.

The Harsh Realities of Guardianship

Over the years, and in nearly every state in America, patterns of abuse have evolved into relatively simple to follow policies—a playbook—that no longer raise red flags. Court insiders consider these policies the norm in regard to conducting guardianships. These protocols include:

- the triggering of a guardianship proceeding.

- the nullification of a ward's *advance directives*, which provide a ward's family, doctors, and lawyers evidence of his prior wishes should he become unable to make or communicate his own decisions. (These directives typically include documents such as powers of attorney, healthcare proxies, and living wills.)

- the preferential selection of a guardian.

- the evaluation, consolidation, and management of a ward's assets.

- the management of a ward's healthcare and medication.

- the determination of who gets paid and how much—based on the "best interests" of a ward—which are unilaterally determined by a guardian and approved by the court.

- the process of turning real estate, hard assets, or life insurance policies into cash—once the actual cash reserve has been exhausted—in order to pay guardianship costs and lawyers' fees.

- the ability of a guardian to have his position terminated if his ward is still alive once all assets have been depleted and the guardianship is no longer profitable.

- the placement of a ward under public funding once his estate has been drained.

Court insiders are experts at finding new ways to extract even more money and assets at almost every stage of guardianship. Many of these "tricks of the trade" are examined in Parts 2 and 3 of this book. If a family wishes to protest guardianship proceedings, the guardian may hire a defense lawyer, who will be fully paid from the estate of the ward. This possibility is discussed, along with the options family members may have, in Part 3.

The following chapters reveal a system that is self-monitored, treats its wards with no regard to their constitutional rights, ignores the end-of-life wishes of its victims, and proceeds in the fashion of the olden-day courts of equity, skirting established law. It is a system of "protection" of the elderly who have done well for themselves that is anything but protective. It is time for it to be exposed to the light of day for the sake of the innumerable wards currently trapped by the courts, those at risk of being swept into this abyss, and the friends and relatives who feel helpless and hopeless.

CONCLUSION

As we have discussed, the history of adult guardianships can be traced back thousands of years, and to a great degree, mirrors the societies that have created them. In the United States, we pride ourselves on having a court system firmly based on the law of the land. It seems, however, that when a guardianship proceeding occurs, those involved are shocked and surprised to find that the unexpected power of the court can destroy a family emotionally and economically; that the entire assets of a ward may be used to enrich others; and that there is little that may be done to stop this process. In such proceedings, the rights of individuals and their families are often set aside and ignored by guardianship courts of "equity."

What we will come to see is that the equity-based guardianship systems that exist in each state today have been perverted. Rather than protecting a ward of the court, they have become an industry to empower and enrich not only the state but also court insiders who, under the protection of the court, are able to sidestep the very laws that were intended to protect the vulnerable in our society. And as you will come to see, the heavy-handed abuses carried out each day in these guardianship proceedings are done so to the advantage of the insiders who benefit most from the industry, with the blessing of the courts.

If you are a family member living in quiet desperation as you watch a relative's estate disappear under the leadership of a court and its guardians, it is time to understand what is happening to you and your loved one. By learning about these systems, you will be better prepared to face what may lie ahead. In the next chapter, we will look at the elements involved in a guardianship proceeding.

2

What Triggers Guardianships?

"A trap is only a trap if you don't know about it.
If you know about it, it's a challenge."
—CHINA MIÉVILLE, WRITER

At the age of eighteen, a person is legally considered an adult. The law generally assumes that adults are capable of making decisions regarding their own lives, be they financial, social, or legal. But sometimes a person who would otherwise be considered an adult loses the capacity to make such judgments due to an illness or condition that makes decision-making impossible, or limits her understanding or appreciation of her actions and their consequences. When this occurs, someone may have to step in to protect the interests of the individual who has lost "capacity."

Whether this substitute decision-maker is a family member, friend, or stranger depends on the directions contained in a person's end-of-life plan. To complicate matters, different people may have different ideas about what is in the best interests of a loved one, even if they all have that person's well-being in mind. Sometimes, the person who has lost capacity does not realize it or resists attempts to take away her autonomy.

Consequently, the appointment of a guardian for an adult can be a stressful, confusing, and guilt-ridden time for all concerned.

Because the guardianship industry operates so far under the radar by design, it is unlikely that the average individual would even know that this process exists, let alone possess the knowledge and information necessary to trigger it.

Normally, when specific circumstances or concerns arise about a person who requires serious intervention—like concerns over their potential for abuse or vulnerability—one might contact a lawyer or agency to inquire about what can be done to determine how to best help someone they believe is in need of assistance or protection. Depending on the input provided, that lawyer or agency might quickly recommend that a guardianship action—called an *incapacity determination* in many places—take place immediately to protect the loved one.

To the average individual, the term "incapacity" is vague and threatening, while the term "guardianship" evokes feelings of protection and safety. It sounds like a reasonable and effective means to deal with the thorny issue of helping a vulnerable person. But the average individual is likely not aware—unless it becomes personal—of the immensely complex details and legal ripples created by initiating the guardianship process, and what it all means to the person being evaluated as well as everyone else involved. Once the course of action starts, it is overwhelming and very difficult to stop. The initial phase of this legal procedure often involves specific and predictable triggering scenarios.

NINE COMMON TRIGGER SCENARIOS

To illustrate how guardianships begin, let's consider the following nine common scenarios (of course, there are others) taken from real life, all of which have served as triggers for taking actual elderly individuals into guardianships. These scenarios demonstrate that guardianships come about for a variety of reasons—some benign, some sinister, some from family, and some from others, but all ending with a vulnerable person being placed under the control of a total stranger and having all her rights stripped away.

SCENARIO ONE
A Dispute in the Family

A man has lived a successful life with his wife and has dutifully made plans for their golden years. These plans include advanced directives, a will, a power of attorney, and a healthcare power of attorney. He and his wife have two grown children: a son, who lives in the same city; and a daughter, who lives out of town and has kept her distance from her parents. To make sure that his wishes are carried out, the man has shared his formal end-of-life plans with his son, whom he sees often, but not with his daughter, whom he rarely sees.

The man suddenly takes ill and dies, leaving his wife to execute his plans. The son takes on the responsibility of caring for his aging mother based on his knowledge of and adherence to the plans made by his father. Then the daughter abruptly appears on the scene. She is concerned that she may not have been included or treated equally to her brother in her father's documents. When her brother tries to adhere to the father's wishes without involving his sister, she accuses him of having undue influence and stealing from their father's estate. Whether or not these claims have any basis in fact, she hires an attorney to protect her interests. Her attorney files a motion with the court to initiate an incapacity hearing, which ultimately leads to guardianship of the mother—the executrix of the father's estate. As a result, all the father's assets are frozen.

SCENARIO TWO
Concern for the Dissipation of a Ward's Money

An elderly but wealthy widow lives alone and is somewhat forgetful. She is fortunate enough to find someone she loves and wishes to spend the rest of her life with. Her children, however, are suspicious that their mother's money is going to her new lover at their expense. They hire an attorney, who makes a motion for incapacity, effectively freezing their mother's assets and protecting them from being improperly taken or dissipated by the new man in her life.

Scenario Three
Guardianship as a Weapon of an Angry Spouse

After many years of unhappy marriage, a couple's relationship begins to reach its breaking point. The husband contemplates filing for divorce. After speaking to his attorney, he is told that divorce could be a costly process. Instead, the husband alleges that his wife's behavior has become erratic. He claims she has been making unwise decisions and wasting money due to mental incapacity. Since an incapacitated person has no rights to sue or hire legal counsel, the husband arranges for his wife to be placed under professional guardianship, which allows him to avoid the expense of divorce.

The pathway to this outcome involves reporting unusual behavior to law enforcement. It could be something as simple as being unable to pass a sobriety test, or anything that is easily construed as the behavior of an incapacitated person. In many states, law enforcement has the right to detain such an individual and place her under observation in a mental health facility for as long as twenty-four to thirty-two hours. This lawful action is known as *involuntary commitment.*

What the husband is not considering in this scenario is that his wife can counter-claim spousal abuse due to mental illness, which is nearly impossible to refute. This allegation can lead to the process of guardianship of the husband as well. And in this high-stakes game, it is entirely possible that the system will take away control from both parties by putting each of them into guardianship. Each of these legal actions is taken by attorneys, who supposedly represent the best interests of the spouses. It is a convenient way for attorneys to take full control of their clients and every aspect of their lives, including their assets.

Scenario Four
A Family's Honest Attempt to Get Help for a Loved One

Three adult children notice the deterioration of their mother's behavior and seek advice from an attorney about what is best for her. The attorney suggests guardianship. Trusting the system and their lawyer, the children agree, expecting the court to create a situation in which their mother is safe and her needs are taken care of fairly and justly, perhaps by family with help from the court. What the children may not be aware of is that it will be the court-appointed guardian alone who will make all the decisions in regard to their mother, possibly disregarding family members' concerns or financial interests.

Scenario Five
A Non-Family Member Recognizing a Need for Assistance

A neighbor is aware that the elderly widow who lives alone next-door gets very few visitors. In addition, beyond not looking well and acting strangely, she seems very suddenly to be getting lost in the neighborhood she's lived in for years. The concerned neighbor seeks help for the widow, but unbeknownst to him, the widow's condition is temporary and merely the result of a reaction to an antibiotic she has been taking for an infection, which has almost been eliminated.

Nonetheless, as a good citizen and neighbor, he calls the Department of Adult Protective Services to report a vulnerable elderly person. An urgent assessment is made by a case officer, and it is determined—as his training strongly suggests—that an intervention should be immediately undertaken. Even though the symptoms of her adverse drug reaction soon disappear, within days an *emergency temporary guardianship* (see "Emergency Temporary Guardianship" on page 69) is created. Typically, there is no attempt to determine the whereabouts of next-of-kin or whether any exist at all. This greatly streamlines the process and allows a permanent guardianship to move forward quickly. Often, children are shocked to learn that their parent has been taken into guardianship without them ever being contacted. Whether or not the widow has siblings or children, from this point on, all care and assets are in the hands of her guardian.

SCENARIO SIX
Intervention of Financial Institutions

An elderly widow worth millions wants to indulge her grandson, whom she loves dearly, with a generous gift to pay for a semester of college. She goes to her bank and asks for a cashier's check for $25,000 made out to the student, who has accompanied her to the bank. On receiving the check, the young man hugs and kisses his grandmother, who returns the favor lovingly.

The bank teller, unaware that the young man is the woman's grandson, remembers reading about how older women are sometimes bamboozled by their pool boys, who may offer affection for money. He calls Adult Protective Services. When they arrive at the widow's home, the grandson has gone home, but the presence of threatening investigators terrifies the widow enough that she is unable to answer their probing questions properly. She is involuntarily committed for her own protection and ultimately placed under guardianship.

SCENARIO SEVEN
Intervention of Medical Institutions

A physician familiar with her longtime patient's easy bruising from the use of aspirin for chronic headaches retires. She is replaced by a new physician, who does not bother to take a thorough history of the patient, but notices multiple bruises all over the arms of this elderly widow. She mistakes them for defensive struggle bruises and assumes her patient is being physically abused.

Physicians and financial institutions are required by law to report evidence of abuse or vulnerability, setting in motion what is many times an unneeded and inappropriate guardianship, particularly when large sums of money are in play. The physician does her duty by calling the authorities, who rush to the doctor's office and interrogate the patient. The elderly woman is terrified and improperly answers some of their questions, resulting in her involuntary commitment, which is then followed by an incapacity hearing.

SCENARIO EIGHT
Family Members Fear the Loss of Their Inheritances

A dedicated daughter has been caring for her elderly father without the help of other family members. She has been thriftily spending her father's money on things she cannot herself provide for him. The work has drained her energy and resources and, despite wanting to take care of her loved one, the job has proven too difficult for one person to perform by herself.

The daughter now seeks assistance and respite from family members, who are unsympathetic or unappreciative of the work being done for their relative. The caregiver then seeks help from the court to provide a higher level of care with outside help or even institutionalization by requesting she be appointed as her father's family guardian. This would formally free up funds for his increasingly costly care.

Her siblings hear of the move and fear their inheritance is at risk, so they oppose the proposal on the grounds of undue influence by the caregiver and disparage her. The court does not know whom to believe or favor. This allows the court to rule in favor of a professional guardianship rather than a family one.

SCENARIO NINE
Law Enforcement Intervention

Involuntary hospitalization for mental observation and evaluation is a very effective shortcut to imposition of involuntary guardianship in many places. In Florida, this is enforced under the Baker

Act; in California, by the Lanterman–Petris–Short (LPS) Act. This law enforcement process authorizes a qualified law enforcement officer or clinician to involuntarily confine a person suspected (with no due process) of having a mental disorder that might make her a danger to herself or others to a mental facility without her consent for a period of usually several days. During this time in a locked-down mental ward, the person being confined is typically housed with seriously mentally ill people and heavily medicated with controller drugs, which are often injected to assure results. Then she is taken—overmedicated, isolated, and without counsel—to face a judge, who will immediately determine whether she should be placed under guardianship.

Among behaviors that qualify for this treatment are walking unsteadily (the assumption and excuse is alleged drunkenness), slurring of speech or altered consciousness (assumption and excuse is drug or alcohol abuse), or any behavior that is out of acceptable norms in the opinion of the law enforcement officer. While any of these scenarios could be caused by any number of benign conditions that would not require such draconian intervention, these potential wards—regardless of their underlying condition—are very lucrative and low-hanging fruit for the imposition of guardianships.

CONSEQUENCES OF GUARDIANSHIP

The nine scenarios I have presented to you are by no means the only ways that guardianships are triggered. There is, however, one common element present in most involuntary professional guardianships: The people who trigger the process are painfully unaware of and totally unprepared for the consequences, complications, and concerns that guardianship brings.

Guardianships have a start, middle, and end. No matter the trigger, a guardianship is complex, intrusive, and driven by a legal process that is foreign to the average individual and difficult to comprehend. At the start, families with any pre-existing degree of dysfunction are forced to deal with the very real threat that a loved one and her assets—the rightful inheritances of members of her family—may become the property of a professional guardian. The embarrassment and pain of having a loved one declared incapacitated as a result of triggering a court proceeding—as well as the family feuds over money and power that may follow—are major blows to all concerned. And not knowing what is going to happen to your loved one is a terrible thing to contemplate.

CONCLUSION

To paraphrase the late congressman Claude Pepper, "guardianship is the most severe verdict our legal system can reach short of the death penalty." Guardianships are far too easy to start and far too difficult to end. It can be just a matter of days from the time someone contemplates triggering a guardianship to the time that a vulnerable but innocent individual becomes a ward of the state with no rights or assets, fully under the control of a total stranger, who knows nothing about her preferences, religion, family, or life.

Even the most ardent supporters of guardianship recognize that, even under the best of circumstances, it is a life-altering situation that is almost always terrifying for all involved—except for those who act as professional guardians for a living. The following chapter describes the middle part of guardianship and the court system responsible for the guardianship industry.

3

The Equity
Court Structure

*"Discourage litigation. Persuade your neighbors to
compromise whenever you can. Point out to them
how the nominal winner is often a real loser in fees,
expenses, and waste of time. As a peacemaker,
the lawyer has a superior opportunity of being
a good man. There will still be enough business."*

—ABRAHAM LINCOLN

Guardianship proceedings can be extremely complex and the enormous power placed in the hands of the presiding judges can be difficult to comprehend. Proceedings are statutory, and imposition of guardianship is supposed to be a last resort according to almost every state statute.

A good example is Illinois statute 755 ILCS 5/11a-3 and 3b, which states, "Guardianship shall be utilized only as is necessary to promote the well-being of the person with a disability, to protect him from neglect, exploitation, or abuse, and to encourage development of his maximum self-reliance and independence. Guardianship shall be ordered only to the extent necessitated by the individual's actual mental, physical, and adaptive limitations."

Sadly, it often turns out to be the preferred and first choice of probate judges, especially in guardianship "hotspots"—places where the majority of cases occur—across the country. From their chambers, judges push all the buttons that orchestrate the many players in a guardianship drama.

THE POWER OF PROBATE

Especially confusing for the uninitiated who witness or are involved in these proceedings is the fact that probate court does not function like the courtrooms we see on television. Unlike criminal courts or civil courts, where due process holds sway and juries function, guardianships are initiated in equity courts. As we have seen, these courts evolved from English law. Although many of them have been included in the totality of a given state's judicial system, they continue to function in relative secrecy and isolation, immune from the normal safeguards and checks and balances present in other courts.

The courts in question have chancery (equity) powers, which were intended to be extremely limited. They are bound by both their individual state's documents and the foundational documents of the country, which include the Constitution and the Bill of Rights, which further limit the jurisdiction of such courts to impose guardianship by the Fifth and Fourteenth Amendments. Despite all these intended limitations and restrictions, according to a report in *Forbes,* "It is difficult to impossible to know how many people are under guardianship or conservatorship in the United States. . . . Many states do not do comprehensive record-keeping. A 2013 AARP report gave a 'best guess' estimate of the number of adults under guardianship nationally at 1.5 million, but added the data 'are scant and vary in quality.'"

Since guardianship is by far the most serious deprivation of civil and human rights after slavery—as it impedes and fully erodes the ability of an individual to exercise his rights or use his property—protecting and maintaining the basic civil rights of wards in a court that routinely strips them away is a serious issue in probate. These rights include due process, roughly defined as

"Notice of Hearing," which refers to legal documents issued by the court in order to inform individuals that the government is pursuing action against them. So important are Notices of Hearing that, in July 1992, Congress added additional safeguards for potential elder abuse by enacting the Americans with Disabilities Act, which is at least intended to protect the elderly and disabled by further reducing the imposition of rights-robbing court outcomes.

HOW ARE PROBATE COURTS CONSTITUTED?

To better understand the nature of the courts handling adult guardianship cases, it is helpful to understand how these courts are put together—specifically, how most judges are selected to serve on the bench. While each state has its own laws guiding how judges are chosen, the following reflects the general process used.

Every state government consists of three branches: executive, legislative, and judiciary. The judiciary is typically the only independent branch of government and designed to be free of political influences. Generally speaking, all state courts are under hierarchical supervision of the state supreme court, and in particular, the chief justice of the state supreme court. The chief justice is responsible for and delegates authority to circuit courts. All state courts are funded on an annual basis through the legislative budget process.

State circuit courts are administered locally by a chief judge appointed by the state supreme court. This judge is responsible directly for all cases determined in a particular circuit, including criminal, civil, and equity matters such as family courts, divorce courts, bankruptcy courts, and of course, probate. Often in larger circuits, a chief judge for a probate division is named. Most probate judges are elected or retained in a normal election rotation. They may run as members of a political party to which they retain fealty. It is common for supporters of a given judicial candidate to create and fund campaigns for that candidate. A significant portion of the election or reelection campaign funding in probate races typically come from attorneys and guardians who practice as well as appear in a given judge's courtroom on a regular basis.

Once elected—or reelected, as is typically the case—the judge may have the latitude to recruit and select his own staff as positions open up, but the backbone of workers in the court are civil servants whose tenure in the court can be far longer than any given judge. While they may serve at the judge's pleasure, their often not-so-subtle attitudes and opinions can influence judicial outcomes, and often do.

Probate Standards of Proof

The three primary court standards of proof are, in descending order of difficulty: proof beyond a reasonable doubt; clear and convincing evidence; and preponderance of evidence. The evidence for a claim of incapacity has to meet only the middle standard clear and convincing evidence, making the creation of wards easier with a judge's very wide discretion and latitude to fashion remedies. A judge has complete latitude to establish a guardianship based solely on his assessment of the "facts" of a case as presented by a court insider, even if there has been no investigation of the allegations that precipitated the case.

Probate Rules

In many states, there is a parallel set of rules by which the court should function called "probate rules." These rules are compiled by attorneys practicing in the field of probate and published for consumption by the legal community. It is important to recognize that there are often conflicts between statutes and the probate rules. In these situations, probate rules supersede state statutes.

A discrepancy about a single word in either the statutes or probate rules can trigger a judge's decision to default to the rules rather than the statutes. For example, the probate rules might employ the word "surrogate" in referring to a litigant in the position of healthcare power of attorney, but the statute might use the words "healthcare power of attorney" to refer to the same person. If there is litigation about the healthcare power of attorney, a judge, with his enormous latitude to make decisions, can use the word surrogate, if he so chooses, to support the argument of those he has deemed the "good guys," and to use against those he regards as the "evildoers."

Probate is a non-criminal, administrative state court functioning as a court of equity. It does not usually employ or seat juries, although in some states, the allegedly incapacitated person is entitled to a jury—if the judge allows it. It is supposed to follow *due process*, the absolute right to adequate notice and hearing. But because equity can sometimes rely on additional consideration to statutes, many states have a parallel system of unique rules that can supersede statutes when there is a conflict between statutes and probate rules. Probate functions by the issuance of writs to accomplish the administration of estates (i.e., the settlement of a deceased's estate, paying off debts, and distributing assets to heirs). In many states, it is called the Widow's and Orphan's Court. The state's legislature limits or augments jurisdiction of the probate division.

The major non-guardianship focus of probate is the judicial process by which a dead person's debts are settled and estate property is valued, beneficiaries are determined, an executor or fiduciary in charge of estate distribution is declared, and ultimately the possession of the estate and its assets are legally transferred to the court-determined beneficiaries. The basic role of the probate court judge, whose opinion is absolute, is to assure that the deceased person's creditors are paid, and that any remaining assets are distributed to the proper beneficiaries.

Probate courts are also arbiters of the formal, statutory guardianship process, in which an estate and control of its now incapacitated, legally dead originator—the ward—are transferred to court-appointed fiduciaries (guardians, conservators) until such time as the ward either expires or recovers from his mental, physical, or other relative disability. In order to gain proper jurisdiction, or the legal authority for a court to exercise its authority over a person or an estate and its living originator, the probate court must strip the incapacitated person of his civil rights, making him a ward, and thus allowing probate control over the disposition and ultimate distribution of his assets.

The mere act of the court exercising any authority over the civil or human rights of the allegedly incapacitated person is to deprive him of one or more of his rights, privileges, and immunities protected by state and federal constitutions. Thus, by statute, the honest probate judge is required to exercise the strictest standards of proof and concern, even though courts can get away with anything when those whom they harm are unable or unwilling to stand up against the abuse. There are many reasons, including PTSD and financial insecurity, why victims of legal abuse are unable or unwilling to stand up for themselves.

Even after a ward expires, his estate may be, and often is (in contentious cases), passed not to the heirs named in a will or trust but to a probate-appointed curator, who is a temporary caretaker of the assets, and then to another court-appointed representative of the estate for ultimate distribution to valid heirs of whatever remains after payments of all debts and fees.

When a guardianship expires because of the death of a ward, it must be settled before a proper probating of the decedent's estate can begin. This is another opportunity for additional litigation and fees. In the one instance where a guardian can be held accountable to the estate, a guardian who acts improperly in the opinion of the judge who appointed him may be surcharged for his behavior (the equivalent of paying a hefty fine).

Probate cases can be either *adversarial,* involving opposing sides, or *non-adversarial,* meaning all parties work in cooperation to reach the best resolution for everyone. Cases are assumed to be non-adversarial unless declared to be adversarial early in the proceedings. Contested guardianships where there is opposition to the appointment of a guardian are adversarial and may involve protracted litigation.

HOW DO PROBATE COURTS FUNCTION?

The machinery of a court exists to create a workflow for a judge and all who support him. Matters are usually brought to the attention of a court by motions or pleadings from attorneys who are officers of the court representing their clients. These matters constitute the *docket* (judicial schedule) for a judge. Decisions on the merits of the pleadings are the way courts make their rulings known in writing. Judges, lawyers, and to a certain extent, guardians practicing in probate courts all enjoy judicial immunity to one degree or another, meaning that they cannot be sued except for egregious violations of ethics or rules.

Probate courts cannot issue arrest warrants or search warrants. A probate court can hold an individual in contempt, sanction litigants for abuse of process, and issue bench warrants to bring someone before a judge to explain why he has not complied with a previous summons.

What Do Probate Judges Rule On?

The probate guardianship system concerns itself with:

- the capacity of an allegedly incapacitated person.
- the degree of a ward's vulnerability to exploitation.
- the need for guardianship.
- the choices for fiduciaries.
- the prior wishes of an allegedly incapacitated person.
- monitoring a ward, his estate, professional fees, and reports.
- the ultimate distribution of what remains of an estate.

Sixth Amendment Issues

In criminal trials, the Constitution guarantees that parties are assured of a fair trial, a speedy trial, and a juried trial, as well as counsel, presumption of innocence, the right against self-incrimination, and the Double Jeopardy Clause, which refers to being prosecuted more than once for the same offense.

None of these promises necessarily applies in state equity guardianship courts. Fairness might be in the eye of the beholder, but speedy trials in probate courts only happen in the initial rush to create guardianships. After that, prolonged litigation can go on for years, as court dockets are so loaded with cases that hearings are often scheduled months in advance—even in emergency matters or for hearings that might last only fifteen minutes. These delays occur while a ward is under the control of a guardian and his lawyer. With every passing day, exploitation of an elderly ward becomes more unbearable, and his condition may deteriorate rapidly while no one is able to do anything about it. Jury trials almost never happen in guardianship matters. Only rarely are requests for a jury trial granted.

WHAT IS EQUITY?

The term *equity* actually means "fairness." As a legal system, it is a body of law that addresses concerns for relief that fall outside the jurisdiction of common law and employs a particular legal methodology of dealing with certain types of cases with set remedies and procedures distinguished from "legal" ones. Equitable relief is generally available only when a legal remedy is insufficient or inadequate in some way. Equity has been part of our judicial system from the inception of American jurisprudence.

Article III, Section 2, Clause 1 of the United States Constitution enshrined equity into our legal system as the federal judicial power in "all cases, in law and equity, arising under this Constitution, the laws of the United States, and treaties made, or which shall be made, under their authority." But federal law actually provides no relief from probate equity decisions. The so-called "probate exception" forever enshrines the proviso that a federal court lacks jurisdiction over probate.

According to wealthmanagement.com, " . . . the probate exception provides that a federal court lacks jurisdiction to probate a will or administer an estate. In 1946, the Supreme Court (in a case called Markham vs. Allen) clarified the exception and held . . . that federal courts are barred from assuming jurisdiction over res (matters) subject to another court's jurisdiction."

This proviso was originally intended to placate states that were concerned about giving too much power to the federal government, especially in matters of inheritance and slavery. Recall the probate courts ruled on interstate slave trade until 1865. The official rationale is that the federal courts are not designed to be an appellate court for the state courts. For all practical purposes, since 1946, federal courts are barred from assuming jurisdiction over probate and estate matters, leaving the only redress to state appeals courts.

The Crucial Difference Between Equity and Law Courts

As described in Chapter 1, in olden days, there used to be two different courthouses: one of the court of law (the King's), and one of equity (the Church's). Eventually, the courthouses were consolidated, and a single judge could hear each type of case. The disparate matters and courts of law and equity still exist to this day, even though on the surface most states have combined these different processes into one court system for the sake of convenience.

Two different court systems continue to function today in America, and the distinction can be significant. Specifically, a court of law must follow the "black letter" (basic and unbendable) rules, such as due process, rules of evidence, and jury availability, as well as adhere to the technical constraints that allow the people to have faith in their courts.

But, uniquely, a court of equity, when run by court insiders, may rely on nothing more than a judge's perceptions of what is equitable, fair, and equal—his discretion. No juries allowed.

Everything, including what evidence to admit or ignore, which case law is relevant or not, and whom to believe or not, is strictly based on a judge's opinion, even though this is patently illegal. Although a judge's options were intended by law to be quite limited, when an insider scheme raises its ugly head, it creates a litany of judicial anomalies that tarnish the perception of how we view the courts.

Equity cases, including probate, divorce, family, and bankruptcy cases, suffer from a lack of consistent application of pertinent statutes, which seem to be often ignored. These courts have assumed absolute latitude to hear as much or as little of what they consider fair, at the sole discretion of the sitting judge. The outcome is based on subjective impressions and opinion factors, rather than case law, or even common law. In court of law cases, facts are what they are, and you win or lose; in equity cases, a court will fashion almost any remedy it sees fit so that both parties win or both parties lose fairly—at least in theory.

When the lives of our loved ones as well as their estates hang in the balance in a probate matter, it is not so much about what the law says, but what and how much a judge wants to hear. With so much at stake and court insiders at such an incredible advantage by virtue of their familiarity with judges, it should not be surprising that the scales of justice are often tilted in their favor.

CONCLUSION

Probate equity courts are very different from civil and criminal courts of law. They represent a world and a set of rules and procedures totally unfamiliar to the average citizen, who might find himself involuntarily or unwittingly engaged in the guardianship of a loved one. In good guardianships, these courts function as advertised, providing assistance and security to those in need of help when family cannot or will not provide it.

But in countless judicial "hotspots" throughout the country, these courts have spearheaded perversion of the laws intended to protect the vulnerable into a well-oiled, immensely profitable moneymaking machine for their insiders. While there are a lot of people to blame for such court-sanctioned mistreatment, only a judge has the power to allow or stop every bad thing that happens in an abusive guardianship. Absent meaningful supervision or monitoring, the penultimate power of the probate judge can and often does succumb to forces that pollute the equity process and result in unnecessary and fraudulent guardianships and all that they entail.

4

The People in the Guardianship Industry

"Take care of the elderly people."
—LAILAH GIFTY AKITA, WRITER

As we have seen, a guardianship is a legal relationship in which a state court gives one person or entity (the guardian) the duty and power to make decisions regarding personal matters or property for someone who has lost her civil rights by court order after being deemed "incapacitated" and in need of the court's protection (the ward).

The legal removal of an individual's rights is an extreme measure with far-reaching consequences and major repercussions for all concerned. Absent any other reasonable alternative, no one would ever intentionally choose to be a ward with no rights. Consequently, the United States system of guardianship has evolved over the last thirty to forty years into a highly complex legal exercise, a choreographed performance in which there are many officials and moving parts, rules, procedures, participants, and players, each with a different role. Very few non-legal outsiders are acquainted with the people who run this process. But this rarified knowledge of exactly who the players are and what their roles *should be* is an important element in understanding what may lie ahead for a ward and her family.

THE PEOPLE INVOLVED IN GUARDIANSHIPS

From a novice's neutral point of view, each of the roles these people or organizations play appears to have been created for the benefit or protection of a vulnerable ward. Without a clear understanding of all the people who may be involved, it is difficult to know who is responsible for each task in a complex legal system.

Here is a partial listing of individuals who are cogs in the guardianship wheel that you may encounter. It is divided into two categories. The first represents the individuals or groups that may bear direct responsibility for a guardianship being created as well as its functioning. These we call the *court insiders*. The second group is usually composed of those individuals and services hired by a guardian or court to perform required tasks. These are the *ancillary players*.

Law Enforcement

Sometimes guardianships begin when local law enforcement is tasked with detecting and apprehending individuals accused of or suspected of acting in a manner dangerous to themselves or others and subjecting them to involuntary inpatient psychiatric evaluation. These involuntary commitments, known in Florida as the Baker Act, can last for as much as seventy-two hours, and may even be extended under certain circumstances. They typically lead to petitions for incapacity and, ultimately, guardianship. These actions can be precipitated by a formal warrant but most commonly occur from a citizen's complaint or direct observation by law enforcement officers of unusual behavior or actions. Such action might be due to something as simple as being overly intoxicated or as serious as having hallucinations, acting in a threatening manner to another individual, or behaving in any way that seems out of the ordinary and might pose a threat to someone according to the opinion of a law enforcement officer.

Petitioners

These are the people who ask a court to initiate a guardianship evaluation process by reporting to a court what they see, or think they see, happening to an allegedly incapacitated person. Any adult could be a petitioner, but in most cases, petitioners turn out to be family members or their attorneys. These relatives may be close family members or distant ones, related by blood or marriage or adoption, or not related at all.

Departments of Children and Families and Adult Protective Services

The Department of Children and Families (DCF) and Adult Protective Services (APS) are two agencies of state, county, or city government tasked with investigating and receiving complaints of abuse against vulnerable children and adults. Field officers are responsible for visiting alleged victims of abuse and reporting same to their supervisors, which, in turn, initiate reports for action of state attorneys or other agencies for the protection of the vulnerable. This is the official complaint department for guardianship abuse in many states. While such agencies are not part of law enforcement, they do have the ability to activate law enforcement if urgently needed.

Interested Persons

Interested persons are the only individuals who can be recognized by the court to take legal action in a guardianship proceeding on behalf of or against an estate. Any person, relative or not, who has a stake in the outcome of a guardianship—personal or monetary—including potential heirs, is an interested person. If a court determines that an individual is not an interested person, that individual does not receive standing with the court and cannot participate in guardianship proceedings except as an observer or witness.

Wards

Individuals who are being considered for an incapacity hearing are called *allegedly incapacitated persons* (AIPs). By virtue of their disabilities, incapacitated persons are regarded as both a danger to themselves and vulnerable to abuse or exploitation by others. AIPs who are ultimately deemed by a probate court judge to be "incapacitated" subsequently become wards. Recently, court initiatives to find a softer title for an incapacitated person have suggested the term "protected person" be used.

A guardian may be appointed only for a ward and only a ward may have a guardian. Once an AIP is determined to be incapacitated by the judge, she is stripped of her civil rights. The newly minted ward is then placed under the court-approved control of a guardian for her "protection."

Guardians

Guardians, who are sometimes known as *conservators*, are individuals appointed by the court to protect the health, assets, and welfare of a ward. In some cases, a guardian is appointed to oversee only a certain aspect of a ward's affairs, such as the finances of a ward (guardian of the property) or the healthcare of a ward (guardian of the person). These cases are known as *limited guardianships*. In contrast, a *plenary guardianship* refers to the appointment of a guardian who has been granted the right to handle all legal decisions on behalf of a ward. Additionally, guardians may be appointed on a temporary, permanent, or emergency temporary basis. (See "Emergency Temporary Guardianship" on page 69.)

A guardian can be a family member, a court-approved lawyer, or a professional. After a short educational course, family guardians are given authority over a relative, despite their lack of training or health standards, which are usually imposed on professional guardians. In some states, while a family member may be selected as a guardian, the court selects a co-guardian who may be more familiar with the guardianship system. In many instances, these co-guardians are selected from a court-approved list and in many cases are lawyers.

There are also public guardians who care for indigents, as well as private, for-profit guardians who limit their cases to potential wards with significant assets. They bill by the hour or fraction of the hour at court-approved rates. Both are unlicensed people, unrelated to the ward by blood or marriage, who have gone through a training program usually developed and approved by the state guardianship association, passed a state test, and been certified to act as a guardian. In some states, there are continuing education requirements. After having passed their certification examination, these newly minted guardians are free to look for and find potential wards.

Court-Appointed Attorneys for Wards

Despite losing their rights, wards need some legal protection, too. In nearly all states, guardianship laws compel judges overseeing the process to appoint a lawyer to represent the interests of an allegedly incapacitated person. Most states provide for the appointment of legal counsel for an AIP at the outset of proceedings, whether the AIP has a prior attorney or not. In New York, for example, the court routinely appoints an attorney to represent an AIP. This attorney's role is to ensure that a potential ward's point-of-view is presented to the court. These lawyers are trusted by the judge, paid by the hour, often receive multiple referrals from judges, and assume the statutorily-mandated responsibility to represent wards effectively.

At a minimum, the representation should include conducting personal interviews with the person; explaining her rights and counseling her regarding the nature and consequences of the proceeding; securing and presenting evidence and testimony; providing vigorous cross-examination; and offering arguments to protect the AIP's rights.

Guardians' Attorneys

These are attorneys specializing in guardianship law, paid by the hour to represent the interests of a guardian, even if they conflict with the interests of a ward or family. Their fees are accumulated and presented to a judge for approval. The money to pay a private guardian's attorney comes from the assets of the ward. Typically, these attorneys are members of the elder law section of the bar association of a state. They typically comprise majority membership on probate rule committees.

THE PRIME PLAYERS IN "EQUITY" COURTS

It is important to recognize that these individuals do the everyday work for these unique courts, which do not function as standard courts of law. They function as courts of equity. This means that all decisions and writs (judgments) are the decision of just one person, a judge, and based on whatever narrative she accepts as true.

Consequently, the people in this scheme and their relations with the courts, which might help shape a given narrative, may be as important as the law. This is an extremely important issue in that the disposition of a judge can be affected by any number of things—your reputation, your attorney, the opposing attorneys, the guardian, or the judge's level of trust in the probate workers we now describe.

Because legal systems in different states evolved at different times and under different circumstances, it is important to point out that some of the players' titles and tasks may differ somewhat from state to state. But as you read on and begin to understand the roles, responsibilities, and purposes of these players, you should be able to recognize the individuals you are likely to encounter during an adult guardianship process. In addition to the obvious court insiders—the judge, lawyers, and guardians—the probate apparatus is populated by a wide variety of workers and providers.

Elected or Appointed Court Judges and Magistrates

Nearly all judges are elected by the populace and are lawyers or former lawyers. They are the bosses of the probate system. Unelected magistrates, self-appointed officials whose authority is limited to whatever has been granted by statute or specified in the appointment, may also sit in these courts and function as judges. In either case, they are singularly responsible for the decision to create a guardianship, for approving fees paid to guardians and lawyers from the estate of a ward and, importantly, for monitoring and disciplining the guardians they appoint. Judges' support staffs include law clerks, bailiffs, court reporters, and ancillary personnel, in most cases at taxpayer expense.

Honest judges are expected to review all fees and expenses to determine whether these expenditures and fees are for the benefit of a ward. Judges can limit or reduce a payment to either a guardian or attorney at will. In heavily litigated cases, a judge can also impose significant surcharges, sanctions, monetary fees, or fines on any party she feels is not being totally cooperative.

Judges are expected to hold themselves to the highest standard of integrity and to the state's court rules. While the actual language of these rules differs slightly from state to state, the rules for judges and their intent is fairly uniform across the country.

The three most common principles of judges' rules of conduct are these:

1. A judge shall perform judicial duties without bias or prejudice.

2. A judge shall not, in the performance of judicial duties, by words or conduct manifest bias or prejudice, including but not limited to bias or prejudice based on race, sex, religion, national origin, disability, age, sexual orientation, or socioeconomic status, and shall not permit staff, court officials, or others subject to the judge's direction and control to do so.

3. A judge should be faithful to the law and maintain professional competence in it. She should not be swayed by partisan interests, public clamor, or fear of criticism.

All guardianship court decisions fall under the umbrella of judicial immunity. If challenged, they are sent to a higher court only by appeal. Despite a judge's judicial immunity, it is possible to ask her to remove herself from a case if there are valid grounds to do so.

Court-Appointed Guardian Supervisors

There is great disparity in how guardians are supervised from state to state. In New York, the state courts appoint court examiners, evaluators, or private lawyers to oversee a guardian and report to a judge. These individuals are paid for using a ward's funds. To achieve the greatest protection for the estates and affairs of incapacitated persons in the state of Washington, the Certified Professional Guardian Board adopts and implements regulations governing certification, minimum standards of practice, training, and discipline of professional guardians. Indiana has no statewide tracking system or central repository for adult guardianship cases that can be shared by the courts, state agencies, or other service providers. In many guardianship courts throughout the country, clerks audit guardianship files for fraud, overbilling, and financial integrity.

Because guardians are not licensed, there is no disciplinary agency equivalent to the Florida Department of Business and Professional Regulation or the Illinois Department of Professional Regulation, which have the authority to remove licenses if improper behavior arises. Recent legislation has created the Office of Public and Professional Guardians (OPPG) in Florida, which, in theory, functions as a complaint department for guardianships, but its authority is strictly administrative and, as such, severely limited, with its worst available punishment being decertification for a guardian. Some state systems, like that of New Mexico, employ court visitors to report to judges on the conditions of wards. In general, supervision of court-appointed professional guardians has historically been porous and ill-defined throughout the country.

Curators

Curators are lawyers who are tasked with managing an estate between the time of death of a ward, when a guardianships ends, and the time when distribution of a ward's estate to heirs should take place. They report to and function under the protection of the court.

Public Administrators

These are court appointees, usually probate lawyers, who may be asked to distribute a deceased person's estate as its personal representative when no will exists, when no family member is willing and available to serve as executor, or when a will is contested by interested persons. A public administrator also may be appointed to manage a living ward's financial affairs.

Court Monitors

Involuntary adult guardianship is often a contentious affair. There can be understandable feelings of frustration and bitterness on the part of a ward. Family members may be suspicious of a guardian's motives. This is why courts are supposed to use plenary guardianship only as a last resort, when all other less restrictive means of addressing a situation are unlikely to be successful.

Some state statutes provide a way to oversee a guardian and attempt to ensure that a ward is not being abused by allowing the court to appoint a monitor upon the request of an interested party or by its own motion. A monitor cannot be a person with a personal interest in a guardianship case, such as a member of a ward's family. The appointed monitor is given wide latitude to investigate the way a guardianship is being executed so as to report problems and findings to the court.

After such a report is filed with the court, a judge may take any action needed to protect a ward's person or property. This includes requiring assets to be produced, modifying the existing guardian-ship plan, or beginning the procedure to suspend or remove the guardian.

Court Clerks

Court clerks manage all court documents of a case, which can contain thousands of pages, reports, and motions. They distribute cases among judges. In some states, clerks have the authority to investigate suspicious guardianships.

Court Reporter

A court reporter is trained to record all testimony and discussions in court hearings. These court records are part of the legal record of the proceedings along with all deposition records and motions in a case. Interested parties must go through their attorneys to inspect these records. Importantly, in nearly every state in the country, these critical records are sequestered and unavailable to the public or researchers because they are deemed "mental health records." The rationale is that these records might in some way injure or reveal the identity of an individual with mental health issues. This controversial and somewhat contradictory practice implies that incapacity is a mental illness.

Mediators

Mediation is becoming an increasinly popular alternative to guardianship courts. Mediators are appointed by the court in highly contested guardianships in an attempt to mitigate disputes between family members without further litigation. These may be court-approved retired judges or specially trained estate lawyers agreed upon by the interested parties, approved by the court, and paid for by a ward's estate.

Examining Committees, Investigators, and Attorneys *Ad Litem*

Courts must gather and rely on some evidence of incapacity. States vary greatly in how they acquire it. In New York and Florida, committees of examiners, which must have at least one member who possesses a doctor of medicine (MD) degree, evaluate allegedly incapacitated persons and report their findings directly to the court. Any dissenting minority opinion is thrown out. Examining committee members recommend court action based on the presence or absence of incapacity, as well as on the degree of incapacity if determined to be present. Judges are not compelled to comply with these recommendations, although it is rare that they do not agree with them.

In states such as Texas, however, there is no examining committee. An incapacity determination proceeds through a complex system of incapacity evaluators, including court investigators, attorneys of record, social workers, family members, and attorneys *ad litem*, all of which separately advise judges, who make the ultimate decision in the matter.

WHO EXECUTES THE DAY-TO-DAY ISSUES OF A WARD?

Guardianships are complicated, and to do their jobs, guardians require multiple complex skills. In addition to the in-court side of guardianship and all its complexities, there are a myriad of other issues that may crop up outside the court on a daily basis. Since guardians are not required to have any particular expertise, it is commonplace for them to employ paid professionals in various fields to inform the decisions they must make for—and at the expense of—their wards. Oftentimes, a service or individual providing a ward with valid and valuable care is replaced by one more favorable to a guardian but providing the identical service.

Caregivers

The term "caregiver" describes an individual who, whether paid or voluntary, renders direct personal services to a ward. These services include but are not limited to assistance with daily living, cooking, cleaning, transportation, and interacting with family members. The employment arrangements for caregivers may be agreed upon by family members or imposed irrespective to the family wishes by a guardian with the consent of a judge.

Social Workers

Clinical social workers advocate for others to better their quality of life. In the guardianship system, they work as the interface between caregivers and the guardians who employ them. These are individuals with either a bachelor's or master's degree in social work who, in most states, must complete many hours of supervised fieldwork in a clinical setting before becoming licensed or certified by the state. In the guardianship system, social workers are employed by guardians and guardianship companies to visit wards and report back to guardians on issues or concerns that may arise. A visit by a social worker is typically billed as a guardian visit at a guardian's hourly rate and paid for by the estate. The frequency of these visits can be as little as once a quarter in many states, or as often as once a week or more at a guardian's discretion.

Financial Advisers

Guardians often handle large amounts of money and make complex financial decisions, including disposition of property, filing tax forms for a ward, day-to-day management of finances, and investment decisions. It is therefore not surprising that there are a number of financial experts involved in guardianships, including:

- Appraisers
- Accountants
- Bank officials
- Financial auditors

- Forensic accountants
- Insurance company representatives
- Investment advisers and brokers
- Property analysts
- Real estate agents
- Tax preparers

Typically, this group of advisers is used repeatedly by the same guardians in most, if not all, of their cases. Sources of recurrent revenue in guardianships generally include social security benefits, IRAs, and pension plans.

Health-Related Professionals

Guardians typically assume responsibility for the health and well-being of their wards. Consequently, guardians maintain relationships and do business with professionals in the medical industry, including:

- Hospitals

- Doctors

- Nurses and nursing assistants

- Residential facilities (skilled nursing facilities, assisted living communities, rehab centers)

Social workers and healthcare facility employees are responsible for maintaining the welfare of a ward and reporting issues to the appropriate authorities. In nursing homes and, in particular, hospitals, administrators and staff who interact minute-to-minute with a ward are generally legally required to follow the instructions of a guardian. As an example, a guardian can restrict the visitation rights of family members to a ward. Hospital staff will be obligated to enforce the restriction, even resorting to the summoning of law enforcement to the facility to prevent family visitation if necessary.

Pharmacy workers, including registered pharmacists and pharmacy technicians, are responsible for assuring that medications properly ordered by physicians or physician assistants are properly compounded, packaged, and delivered to the facility for consumption by a resident. Sometimes, a ward is treated by personal caregivers, who administer to her basic needs, such as eating, bathing, and administration of medication on a daily basis. It is not unusual for a ward's medical care to be transferred from her familiar caregivers to new ones, including physicians and dentists, at the discretion of a guardian, simply for the guardian's convenience.

Estate Handlers

Nationally, guardians control many billions of dollars in property, from automobiles and houses to jewelry and art. They retain the ability to liquidate assets in order to raise cash to the supposed benefit of a ward. When cash assets are in danger of running out and, in particular, when there are large legal or guardian bills to pay, other assets like real estate, jewelry, automobiles, works of art, or expensive silverware may be sold with court approval to the highest bidder to ensure payment. It should not be surprising that guardians maintain close ties and often do business with the following:

- Antique stores
- Art galleries
- Jewelers
- Real estate appraisers and auditors
- Realtors
- Resale shops
- Used car salesmen

Thanks to the ability of a guardian to drain her ward's assets, each of the recently referenced entities benefits from a recurrent stream of business. There is little to no required reporting or judicial oversight of these businesses' charges or transactions.

Professional Appraisers

In order to process a ward's inventory for equality in distribution or for sale, it becomes necessary to assign value to a wide variety of assets. Some assets, such as stocks or bonds, can be easily valued with readily available references. Others, like artwork, jewelry, heirlooms, or even real estate, are more difficult to value. Personal items, such as family photos, may be priceless to one person and worthless to another. Enter a professional appraiser, hired by a guardian, to whom she reports and by whom she gets paid.

THE ROLE OF FAMILY IN GUARDIANSHIPS

The presence of family—or lack thereof—is a prominent feature in guardianships. But in contested guardianships, family is often on the outside of the process looking in, with very little control. Families may make valiant attempts to overturn or fight abusive guardianships or guardians, but they are prevented from communicating directly with these parties, permitted to do so only through attorneys. Even the most trivial communication involves significant legal fees, which quickly mount to punitive amounts.

In far too many cases, retribution from a court for opposing a guardianship generates sanctions and contempt of court monetary fines and, worst of all, forced isolation from the loved one by virtue of a *Stay Away Order*. Stay Away Orders essentially mute dissent from a family by threat of arrest if these orders are violated. Thus, families are relegated to the status of horrified observers, having no ability to intervene on behalf of their loved ones except through tedious, expensive, and often pointless legal maneuverings.

Who Gets the Money When a Guardianship Ends?

If there is any money left in the estate after a guardianship, you might presume that it would automatically default to the proper heirs. This is not the case. Rather, a guardian applies to be the personal representative of the estate, entitling her, in some states, to as much as 3 percent of the estate.

After the death of a ward, which technically ends a guardianship, there is often any combination of outstanding legal fees, claims against the state, tax issues, liens or encumbrances, non-cash assets to be divided, and property to be sold. It is, of course, a court-appointed fiduciary, whether a guardian, curator, or another type of attorney, who handles these matters for a cut of the pie.

The usual process that occurs in probate court in its more traditional role of closing estates of the deceased does not occur in guardianships. In guardianships, this process is hybridized, complicated, and prolonged to make sure that no monies distributed from an estate reach legitimate heirs until each and every one of its outstanding bills—especially guardian and legal fees—have been paid in full. Because court-appointed fiduciaries make more money by pushing papers and motions, the more work done and the more time it takes, the better the reimbursement becomes for these court insiders. Consequently, it can be many years before heirs receive anything, provided there is anything left to receive. In states like Texas, the court immediately reduces the estate by grabbing 3 percent at initiation of a guardianship and another 3 percent of what is left at its termination.

The point is, once the court gets its hands on an estate, not only will the probate process be painful, but even after a guardianship is over, the people who populate the equity probate court will be enriched by the remaining administrative, legal, guardianship, or court fees associated with the estate before a penny is given to anyone else. Americans Against Abusive Probate Guardianship has documented many cases in which this delaying tactic has been used to drag the process along for years.

CONCLUSION

The guardianship industry is populated by a dizzying array of individuals and organizations. Each one plays a defined role in a system that is intended—on paper—to protect vulnerable people. Each one profits in some way from a ward's estate, as well as from dissenting family members. Each one is likely to be totally foreign to a ward and her family, yet they all have a hand in the way a loved one is treated and dealt with in guardianship. The sheer number of unfamiliar people in this system can be overwhelming. To both ward and family member, it is like suddenly entering an entirely new, bizarre universe in which she has no familiarity or control. Understanding who the inhabitants of this universe are and what they do, therefore, can prepare those affected by guardianships to deal with their possible consequences or even manage their outcomes.

PART 2

Where It All Goes Wrong

5

Incapacity

*"When you have an individual and everyone that
cares about them at your complete mercy, in your total
control, with no one watching, the opportunities for
skullduggery and profit are endless."*
—ANONYMOUS GUARDIANSHIP VICTIM

What if you discovered that all the plans you had made for the
last years of your life—even for your funeral—were going
to be completely changed without your permission? What if you
found out that the people you thought were going to care for you
in old age would not be doing so, and that everything you owned
would be taken from you? What if you learned you would be
involuntarily taken from your home and family, placed in a facility, and heavily medicated despite all your planning and wishes?
What if you were told you could not visit with your family ever
again? What if there was nothing you or anyone else could do to
stop it all?

These life-and-death questions describe exactly the dire realities faced by seniors who are taken into involuntary guardianships in America. This is why it is so important to understand what
exactly the legal condition of *incapacity* means. What does it take
to judge an individual "incapacitated"? How is this determination

made with certainty? With so much riding on this one word, this one assessment, we need a clear understanding of what constitutes and what qualifies as legal incapacity.

WHAT IS LEGAL COMPETENCE?

Prior to the 1990s, the term used in legal proceedings to describe an individual requiring guardianship was *incompetent*, meaning a lack of competence. What, then, is competence? *Legal competence* refers to the mental ability of an individual to participate in legal proceedings or transactions, and the ability to take responsibility for his decisions and actions. It does not refer to the skills or abilities needed to function in daily life. In other words, someone might not be competent to make a specific medical decision for himself or sign a particularly complex contractual agreement, but he might be perfectly competent to vote or determine his place of residence. Competence is, therefore, an attribute that is *decision-specific*. Proving overall incompetence in regard to the many decisions we make daily is a very cumbersome task—yet it is exactly what courts were asked to do at the time in every guardianship case.

Over the years, incompetence became harder and harder to prove. The burden of proof was set higher and higher and not very many people could be proven to be incompetent. As such, the American Bar Association and other interested parties in the legal system actively pursued a less restrictive term to describe a person in need of guardianship. Ultimately, they arrived at the word "incapacitated." It is important to note that this term is used in a legal, not a medical, capacity. Medical opinions are rarely even considered by the court, outside of those from an examining committee member.

WHAT IS INCAPACITY?

There are many scholarly articles and books, including those written by the American Bar Association, that attempt to define

guardianship is an arduous process that can take many months. Examiners willing to overturn a ward's incapacity determination are rare, and those involved in creating a profitable guardianship are hesitant to relinquish it. Well-paid examiners tend to give judges what they believe they want. Often a judge will prolong the process by granting one right or two rights at a time over a period of months, until finally ending the guardianship officially. These actions give court insiders ample time for hearings, objections, litigation, delays, and stalling to generate even more fees.

EMERGENCY TEMPORARY GUARDIANSHIP

Immediately after a hearing or motion to determine incapacity concludes, a tipping point in the guardianship process is the institution of emergency temporary guardianship. A judge can, based on suspicion or unproven testimony by anyone (including Department of Adult Protective Services officers), order an emergency temporary guardianship to provide a ward immediate protection from predation and exploitation, stripping away his rights for what should be a brief period of time. These emergency temporary guardianships can last from 90 to 180 days in many states.

The Sixth Amendment to the Constitution guarantees the rights of criminal defendants, including the right to a public trial without unnecessary delay, the right to a lawyer, the right to an impartial jury, and the right to know who your accusers are and the nature of the charges and evidence against you. This constitutional guarantee does not apply to non-criminal cases like guardianship. Similarly, the Fifth Amendment states that no one shall be "deprived of life, liberty, or property without due process of law." It does not apply in state non-criminal courts, such as probate courts.

The Fourteenth Amendment refers to the *due process clause*, a requirement to give adequate notice to all parties in a proceeding to assure fairness and transparency as a legal obligation of all states. This should apply to all courts of law, but for reasons that remain unclear, it does not apply in a probate court of equity. In fact, in a recent survey of guardianship victims taken by Americans Against Abusive Probate Guardianship, more than 60 percent of respondents indicated that their abusive guardianships began with an unnoticed emergency temporary guardianship.

CONCLUSION

Bearing the legal status of incapacity is tantamount to losing your place in society, including all your rights and assets, and possibly even your life. Despite the gravity of the situation, courts create examining committees consisting of members whose political standing is acceptable but whose expertise in the complex area of neuroscience may be sorely lacking. Conflicts of interest have occurred in the past, as these committees were once paid only for findings of incapacity.

The plastic nature of the term "incapacity" and the highly complex nature of cognitive function make guardianships extremely easy for a judge to initiate, especially with the fast and efficient tool of emergency temporary guardianship. Especially for those with assets, the presence of even the most minimal defect in cognition is a threat that can quickly lead to being legally deemed incapacitated and placed under professional guardianship.

6

The Judges

"Woe to those who enact evil statutes,
And to those who constantly record unjust decisions,
So as to deprive the needy of justice
And rob the poor of My people of their rights,
So that widows may be their spoil
And that they may plunder the orphans…"
—ISAIAH 10:1

All judges are theoretically under the control of the Chief Justice of the State Supreme Court and must adhere to the state's judicial rules and, of course, to every aspect of the United States Constitution and Bill of Rights. Like other state officials, judges must run for election to hold or retain office. In doing so, judges can be Independent, Democrat, or Republican. In some states, judges are not elected but appointed by the state bar association, of which they are almost always members, as judges typically start as attorneys. As in other courts, it is very common to see attorneys who practice in the probate arena wind up as judges in that very same arena.

Once in the position of judge, this individual functions under what is known as "judicial immunity," which means that, even if she makes mistakes or wrong decisions, as long as they are not criminal ones, she cannot be sued. Judges often sit on the probate bench for multiple terms. During these terms, they are likely to see the same groups of lawyers and guardians repeatedly. It is not unusual for judges to develop personal relationships with members of both groups, nor is it illegal.

HOW DOES A JUDGE RULE?

Typically, probate judges hold hearings in which opposing interested parties present their cases either through attorneys or *pro se*, representing themselves. These hearings are intended to argue cases and make pleadings through scheduled court appearances on aspects of probate matters. Prior notification of these hearings to all interested parties is intended to guarantee fairness and the ability to prepare and study the docket well in advance. Judges can declare their rulings immediately, or can take as long as they choose to rule. Oftentimes, support personnel who prepare cases for a judge are instrumental in advising her on her ultimate decisions.

How Does a Judge Monitor Guardianships?

Judges are very efficient when it comes to moving cases off their dockets and creating guardianships quickly. But the system often breaks down, especially when it comes to the crucial responsibility of monitoring and supervising guardians, which are clear legislative and judicial duties.

Judges do not actually visit wards to perform their monitoring. They rely on written interval reports from guardians to become informed about the condition of wards and estates, inventory of assets, accumulated fees, and other significant proceedings that may have occurred since previous reports. The most important reports are the annual accounting from the prior year and the guardian's "plan of care" for the coming year. In most states, these must be filed within 455 days of the previous report (one year plus ninety days). These forms are typically completed by attorneys for guardians, so they are almost never verified.

At the start of the guardianship, several reports, including the inventory of marshaled assets, annual budget, and others must be filed. Statistics from numerous states indicate that these annual reports are filed on time in less than half of all cases. Furthermore, the system has a fatal flaw, which is that there is almost no way to determine the accuracy of these reports. They are basically guardians telling judges whatever they so choose. The facts and truth could be anything unless there is a court challenge, but since these reports are not shared with family and often sequestered, the likelihood of a challenge is low. The possibility of fraudulent, self-serving guardian reports is obvious.

Defenders of the current court system make excuses for this systemic failure, attributing it to lack of funding. There are not enough funds to pay judges who understand the system and are willing to put in the effort to do their jobs. There are not enough volunteers to do the work. And there is not enough money to pay people to do it. Apologists also claim that courts lack the money for staff to oversee guardians and review the periodic reports they are required to submit.

EX PARTE MEETINGS

In addition to scheduled hearings, judges and lawyers can meet to discuss what might be urgent matters prior to hearings in regularly scheduled blocks of time known as *ex parte*. Typically, no records are kept of such meetings. Theoretically, notice must be given to opposing lawyers prior to these meetings to maintain equal and fair access to judges, but this does not always happen. Far too often, court insiders are granted secret *ex parte* meetings at the drop of a hat and conveniently without ever notifying opposing counsel. These meetings are just one more factor that tilts the playing field in favor of those pushing for profitable guardianship.

There may indeed be a shortage of judges to handle cases of all kinds, including guardianships. Nonetheless, despite not being able to monitor adequately the caseloads they have already created, judges continue to establish new guardianships in record numbers. Since these cases deal with the most vulnerable segment of the population—the elderly or disabled who cannot stand up for themselves—it is a recipe for disaster. The best way to reduce the burden on judges would be for them to create fewer wards, but then this change would interfere with the process of wealth extraction.

THE POWER OF A JUDGE

In civil and criminal courts that employ juries and follow strict rules of evidence and due process, there are safeguards in place that reduce the likelihood of judicial bias. While the opinion of a judge is important in these cases, the constitutional right to be judged by a jury of your peers remains as a safeguard to litigants against personal preferences or positions of a presiding judge.

This is often not the case in probate or other equity courts such as family, divorce, or bankruptcy. In these courts, a case's outcome is the singular determination of a judge, based not only on applicable case law and evidence presented but also her personal bias and experience. This can and often does lead to decisions that are difficult to explain, fly in the face of established law, and violate constitutional and probate court rules.

One example of how judges in probate court can make life very difficult for anyone interested in understanding how the court works is the issue of *sequestration*—keeping court records hidden from the public. Most probate courts claim that incapacity is a mental health issue and, therefore, any information that could possibly identify a person in need of guardianship should be masked and the records locked up or sequestered. Although this is a very debatable issue these days, as we now have a much better understanding of mental health and cognitive function than we once did, it is one tool that judges continue to use to prevent adequate study for statistical purposes or meddling by reporters and family, as well as to hide what actually goes on in these hearings. Some insider-run courts even suppress and sequester dockets of these proceedings.

This issue of hiding dockets in probate courts was exposed recently in New Mexico. Public pressure brought on by AAAPG pointed out that New Mexico statutes prevent exactly this action by the court. When confronted with the fact that this information was being intentionally withheld, New Mexico courts were quick to blame clerks of courts personnel, who were suddenly deemed inadequately trained in procedures. Within a very short time, dockets were released to the public. Their analysis alone has revealed a treasure trove of information, such as secret proceedings and deleted dockets. On February 15, 2018, with input from AAAPG in New Mexico, the New Mexico Legislature passed Senate Bill 19, which will purportedly end the routine sequestration of guardianship court proceedings.

Challenges for Judges

Most probate judges today are faced with enormous and growing dockets. In addition, they have real restrictions on the number of staff members they may employ due to budget cuts across the country. They claim they are overworked, underpaid, and understaffed. Faced with large caseloads, too many of them are prone to be unprepared for cases, unfamiliar with the issues at hand, and all too quick to take shortcuts in regard to critical decisions based on whatever narrative they choose to accept in court simply to clear their dockets.

What is a Cold Judge?

When a judge appears at a hearing without having carefully studied all the issues and is unprepared to make a fully informed ruling, she is referred to as a "cold judge." Society depends on judges being fully prepared and not ruling by the seat of their pants. It is difficult to reconcile facts, laws, testimony, and all the other evidence in any given case. The risk of a cold judge is that critical information may be ignored or disregarded in favor of a decision that is chosen primarily to speed the process and allow the docket to be cleared that much more quickly.

THE INFLUENCE OF THE COURT ENVIRONMENT

Despite being godlike on the bench, judges are human and have relationships with the people they work with. Court personnel and practicing attorneys see judges on a regular basis and interact with them both officially and unofficially, so it is not hard to understand why it might appear to an outsider that there could very well be conflicts of interest for a judge when her friends are practicing in front of her. Personal feelings towards litigants and their attorneys can, consciously or unconsciously, color how the narrative presented to a judge by litigants or interested parties is viewed. It is unavoidable human nature.

Do Judges Display Bias?

Among the many observations in probate matters, it is common to hear complaints that judges tend to label opposing sides as the "good guy" and the "bad guy" in hearings, creating even more division and strife. Decisions and rulings that come seem to follow a pattern based on these labels.

Human nature also comes into play. Biases about any number of factors, including but not limited to demeanor, appearance, race, sex, class, religion, politics, and business relations can have subtle or not-so-subtle influences on a judge. Unlike criminal or even civil cases, in which the burden of proof can vary from preponderance of evidence to beyond a reasonable doubt, in probate courts, the burden of proof depends only on what a judge thinks the preponderance of evidence shows her and no one else.

Can a Judge Be Improperly Influenced?

Probate judges are human and prone to bad habits like the rest of us. Given their absolute power in their court, it is easy to understand how those who know judges well and might be aware of the difficulties they face in their private lives could try to incentivize them to rule in a certain way by virtue of leverage.

There is an endless number of ways to influence another person. And while undue influence is a mighty weapon against families in probate, it does not seem to bother judges when it comes to themselves or their families, or when an influencer is a court insider. Something as simple as a personal favor can be a psychological tool to extract preferential treatment. People in positions of power particularly are exposed to all types of profitable possibilities. Clever people can prey on anyone's weaknesses or habits.

Judges' salaries, while substantial, do not provide these public servants the lifestyles they see in some of the attorneys practicing before them. Augmenting their salaries a bit from time to time or getting in on a great investment opportunity might seem like an understandable choice to make. After serving for a long time, a probate judge may be rewarded by appointment as a federal mediator, which pays significantly better than a judge's salary. Others may be lured to large practices with lucrative salaries, which are justified by reputation and influence on others in the industry.

Are Some Judges Corrupt?

Accusing a sitting judge of corruption takes an enormous amount of courage. The retaliation and blowback can be life-altering. Among victims and families of probate abuse, the question of judicial corruption lingers. It is very easy to understand the motivation of court insiders, who bill by the hour. Clearly it is financial reward—the higher the rate and the more hours, the richer they get. For these downstream vendors, business is business, whether it is with a guardian or anyone else. While a judge may be viewed as the root cause of an abusive or fraudulent guardianship, no one has been able to answer the question of how a judge might profit from declaring a guardianship.

It is easy to see how judges maintain their power and benefit from distributing guardianships to the very people who compose their reelection campaigns and social and professional networks. While it is unseemly, it is not illegal, and, in fact, it is common practice. It is not unlawful for a judge to consort with people she sees in her courtroom. But it is definitely illegal for judges to take bribes or launder money in return for favorable judgments.

In 2016, Janet Phelan, a victim, investigative reporter, and advocate began to look closely at property assessor records in Nevada and other states. She and several colleagues found shocking evidence of a scheme that allegedly explains how judges accept cash bribes that are untraceable.

In short, when money is to change hands, a judge takes out a mortgage on her residence. The amount of the mortgage is slightly more than the expected bribe. After receiving the value of the mortgage and making one or two payments, the mortgage is suddenly paid in full, in cash, by an unidentified third-party. The result of this transaction is that the judge has profited by essentially the full amount of the mortgage she took out. She pays no taxes on this large capital gain (income tax evasion), and since there is no evidence of her acceptance of cash (bribery, money-laundering) from anyone, everyone involved in the deal is insulated from inspection by authorities.

Judges found to be repeatedly taking out large sums of money in the form of property loans on their homes and quickly paying them back could easily represent enrichment from an improper outside source. But when a judge's income is inadequate to serve as the source of these loan repayments, how hard is it to reason that the repayment funds—usually in cash—are coming from somewhere else?

BASIC CONSTITUTIONAL PROBLEMS
WITH PROBATE EQUITY JUDGES

Judicial misconduct is a very problematic and highly controversial topic. As we have seen, there are many conflicts of interests inherent in the probate process, some quite serious. Some, however, are downright illegal, like the functional denial of due process to victims and families. Judges are the root cause of all abusive guardianships. Without their rulings and lack of supervision and monitoring, there would be far less abuse and exploitation, or perhaps none at all.

The following comments about failed due process in probate are by Ken Ditkowsky, a well-known Chicago attorney and advocate:

> Equity is designed first and foremost to follow the law. Judges cannot create "new law" or use the courtroom for personal gain or the gain of colleagues or donors to their campaigns or anyone else. All state statutes are quite comprehensive—they create jurisdictional criteria that depend and insist on the most important American principle of law, due process. So often it is that failure to provide due process that leads to the abuses so common to American probate courts.
>
> In theory, there should be no distinction between "equity" and the "law" because there can be no equity jurisdiction—even in probate—without strict compliance with the law. Any judge who takes a "shortcut" has acted *ultra vires* (beyond his authority) and is, by definition, corrupt. Any judge who has knowingly received, allowed or tolerated any type of inducement, consideration, or remuneration—direct or indirect, trivial or major—that might influence any such decision is a criminal. Period.
>
> Any failure to fully and strictly adhere to the principles of the United States Constitution by any judge is a criminal event! It may not, because of judicial immunity, be prosecutable as a practical matter, but the judge has committed a crime that could and should result in impeachment.
>
> The vexing problem has always been a lack of enforcement. Every judge should know that there is no jurisdiction when due

process is neglected in favor of expediency in the rush to guardianship, as so often happens when:

1. The victim is not served with the summons required by statute.

2. The victim's next of kin are not served with proper jurisdictional notice.

3. A required competency hearing was not properly held.

4. All litigants do not have fair opportunity to present evidence to enter into the court.

The cover-up of judicial misdeeds and constitutional violations by the courts, the attorney disciplinary commission/JQC, and others is even more deplorable. Federal healthcare funds are stolen in the unnecessary and excessive care (an obvious violation of the federal ADA laws) forced upon the ward, allegedly in the ward's "best interests." The corruption/failure of the law enforcement mechanism—or its apathy and failure to perform its duty—have allowed the probate insiders wide judicial latitude to loot countless estates for their own benefit and waste countless dollars of excessive (and therefore illegal) healthcare benefits for which we all pay but which only they control.

WHO DISCIPLINES JUDGES?

Every state has agencies created to ensure judicial oversight. In many states, these are constitutionally mandated, like the Judicial Qualifications Commission, or JQC, in Florida. These agencies are designed to hold judges to the ethical standards outlined in the Code of Judicial Conduct.

There are fifteen members of the JQC. Six members are court judges. Another four are lawyers selected by the Board of Governors of the state bar association. The last five are non-lawyer political appointees chosen by the governor. The members of the JQC are divided into two panels: an "investigative panel," which takes on similar duties as a prosecutor, and a "hearing panel," which acts like a panel of judges reviewing the case.

The JQC is responsible for investigating complaints submitted by alleged victims of judicial misconduct. The hearing panel reviews the cases made against judges, listening to competing arguments from both sides before sending its findings to the Supreme Court. Judges accused of misconduct are often represented by a private attorney. The JCQ can make recommendations for the discipline of an offending judge, but ultimately the final decision rests in the hands of the Supreme Court.

What Are the Risks to a Compromised Judge?

Given that judges have judicial immunity and are almost never reprimanded or removed by their oversight boards, the risks to a compromised judge might seem very low. This idea goes a long way in explaining rulings that make no sense, contradict evidence, and prolong litigation. It would also explain why judges fail to discipline or monitor the guardians they appoint.

Judges might also fail in their duties by virtue of their own declining mental faculties. It is not unheard of to witness what appears to be an incapacitated judge running a probate court. This notion may explain a number of puzzling issues that pop up recurrently in probate matters and lead to overall abridgment of rights.

Can Judgements Be Reversed?

The only alternative for a loved one who is dissatisfied with a judge's ruling is to embark on a lengthy and very expensive appeal of this decision. The likelihood of successful appeal of what is known as a "lower court ruling" is not much, and may not even be heard by an appeals court at all. At the outset, the best odds available to a litigant appealing a judge's decision are fifty-fifty. Although it is beyond the scope of this book, appeals courts themselves present serious obstacles for those who wish to appeal lower court rulings. The judges who typically comprise courts of appeal, which are also arranged by district, are intimately familiar with the judges below them and have had friendships and shared experiences with them in social arenas. Thus, these judges are less likely to be sympathetic to a litigant than to a judge who does not like to be overturned.

Most states have a procedure for aggrieved litigants to submit a plea to recuse, or remove, a judge from a case, but it is typical for a judge to deny such requests, since she has the ability to say that the call for recusal was not legally sufficient. By virtue of this ability, a judge can stay on a case for as long as she wishes.

Can Judges Be Removed from the Bench?

Under extremely rare circumstances, judges have been removed for engaging in unusually deplorable behavior, but generally speaking, they are unassailable.

From 2010 to 2015, the JQC received 3,353 formal complaints (and this number has been rising from year to year), and 99 percent of them were discarded overall. Of these, 86 percent were summarily dismissed without any investigation of any type, only a cursory review by staff. Of the remaining cases that were reviewed, 0.068 percent of the total number (equal to only 10 percent of the total of non-dismissed cases) were formally charged by recommendation of the Supreme Court. Only seven judges have been removed by JQC recommendations to the Florida Supreme Court in the last eighteen years, according to an investigation by the *News Service of Florida*.

CONCLUSION

Equity court judges are given enormous authority and power over fortunes and lives, but they are human. They are subject to the same vices, influences, habits, and foibles as the rest of us. It is a testament to the justice system that most judges maintain their propriety and rein in their biases to give us a court system in which we can entrust our legal protections, and which allows us to retain our faith in the legal system.

But like other professions, there are bad actors in judgeships. The judiciary is expected to self-police, since it is the only independent branch of government. Failure of this system to recognize or admit the possibility that a judge is acting inappropriately results in outcomes that are unacceptable. Failure of the monitoring and supervisory functions of law enforcement allows and encourages injustice to flourish. For litigants in probate court, there is so much at stake, including lives, inheritances, and, in many cases, mental health. There is simply no room for any type of judicial bias or impropriety. The unique conditions found in equity courts are breeding grounds for judicial misconduct that benefits court insiders, especially guardians.

7

The Guardians

*"If anyone ever tried to put me in a guardianship,
I would fight like hell."*
—APRIL PARKS, FORMER NEVADA GUARDIAN

Courts may create wards, but they have no resources to do the work of protecting them or making decisions for them, so they appoint guardians, who are responsible for fulfilling these needs. In a perfect world, guardians, who are given critical responsibility and control over other people's lives, would work hard to solve the problems that led to guardianship in the first place. Instead, the current system of guardianship too often creates new, more burdensome problems, as it affords guardians numerous ways to take advantage of a ward's finances and properties. It fosters an attitude that turns a blind eye to the vast number of schemes employed by guardians and the many downstream players, who take full advantage of the system, knowing there is little downside. As previously mentioned, many modern-day guardianships have become highly profitable sources of income for guardians.

Unlike professionals such as doctors and nurses, who take an oath to ensure their proper behavior, guardians do not abide by any such oath. Unlike lawyers, who must theoretically adhere to bar standards, guardians have no such formal obligations. Most lucrative employment contracts, like the ones high-level athletes negotiate, contain moral clauses, but guardians are held to no such standards. Medical professionals spend large sums of money on continuing education, while guardians typically do not require any form of higher education. Guardians can choose to become nationally certified, indicating a higher level of professionalism, but only a low number of them ever do so.

Guardians answer to almost no one, and often their familiarity and social connections to judges and everyone else in the court system make it easy for them to operate effortlessly and free of concern about retribution for their actions.

WHAT EXACTLY IS A GUARDIAN?

In today's guardianship scheme, a guardian, or conservator, is as a substitute decision-maker—an individual or company authorized legally with so-called *letters of guardianship* issued by a judge to make decisions regarding a ward's life. As discussed in Chapter 4, in a limited guardianship, a judge grants a guardian limited control over a ward's affairs. For example, a guardian might be entrusted with managing only the financial matters or healthcare decisions of a ward. A plenary guardianship, on the other hand, allows a guardian to handle all aspects of a ward's life. Either form of guardianship may be created on a temporary, permanent, or emergency temporary basis. (See "Emergency Temporary Guardianship" on page 69.) Finally, there are three main groups of guardians: public, professional (also known as private or corporate), and family. While certification requirements for each vary across states, the responsibilities associated with the position are the same no matter what kind of guardian you are.

Family Guardians

Family guardians are the largest group of guardians. The court has the option to appoint a family member who is available and willing to take the responsibility of caring for a family member who is, or is about to be, a ward.

Public Guardians

These guardians deal with indigent individuals who have been ruled incapacitated. They make up the second largest group of guardians in this country. They or the companies they work for have been approved by the court to operate in given localities.

Professional Guardians

Also known as private or corporate guardians, these are individuals or corporations that have fulfilled the basic requirements of their particular state to act as guardians of individuals with assets. They are chosen from a list of approved guardians working within a particular area on the basis of prior performance and financial stability. Professional guardians are the group most frequently involved in fraudulent or abusive guardianships.

HOW TO BECOME A GUARDIAN

Despite the incredible responsibility and authority conferred upon them by the courts, it is surprisingly easy to become a guardian. The precise qualifications and requirements differ from state to state, but to generalize, almost anyone over the age of eighteen who has not been convicted of a felony can take a short training course over a weekend, pass a rudimentary test, pay a fee, and become certified as a guardian in his state. Once certified, a guardian is responsible for finding new cases through whatever means he chooses. There are national boards, like the National Guardianship Association, which confer additional status to guardians who are willing to pay an additional fee and take further training courses. No state requires guardians to acquire a license at this time. Requirements for recertification are minimal and involve submitting routine affidavits and a recertification fee to the state agency that certifies them, such as the Department of Elder Affairs.

Public Guardians

The requirements to become a public guardian vary from state to state, but most states require passing a criminal background check and a record free of bankruptcies, plus some sort of educational training. In Missouri, guardians are elected public administrators, while in Illinois, they are appointed by the governor. Guardians in California are licensed through the Department of Consumer Affairs. In Nevada, guardians are accredited by the Department of Business & Industry, which is under the Financial Institutions Division. In Texas, certification is obtained through the Office of Court Administration under the Guardianship Certification Board.

Educational requirements are different in every state. While many states have adopted rules for certification from the National Center for Guardians Certification, most states require a prospective guardian to complete a thirty- to forty-hour internet or junior college-level course and pass an exam based on this material.

Other requirements may include:

- **Age.** At least between eighteen and twenty-one.

- **Education.** From high school diploma to bachelor's degree.

- **Experience.** Two years of practical experience in a related field (nursing, social work, etc.).

- **Testing.** State exams or Center for Guardianship Certification (CGC) certification exam.

- **Oversight and Monitoring.** By judge, judge's clerk, or court evaluator.

- **Background Checks.** Screening for record of felonies or bankruptcies.

Professional Guardians

All professional guardians must fulfill the identical qualifications required of public guardians, including background and fiscal checks. They must also meet the same minimum educational requirements, as well as some requirements for continuing education.

The combination of insider familiarity, lack of accountability, judicial immunity, and greed can lead to professional guardians controlling a large number of wards. While there are limits to this number in various states, it is not unusual for a professional guardian to have dozens of active cases at any time—in some cases, many more than that. It is this unfettered access to numerous estates belonging to wealthy individuals that constitutes the low-lying fruit of the professional guardianship money grab.

Family Guardians

Family guardians must pass age and educational requirements set by the state. These guardians are held to a lower standard than others. Typically, they are required to complete no more than an eight-hour course on their duties and responsibilities, if even that. No post-course testing is usually needed. It is important to note, however, that family guardians, despite their minimal training, are required to comply with all aspects of guardianship reporting in the same manner as a professional guardian. Depending on the state, family guardians may or may not need to post a fiduciary bond.

HOW ARE GUARDIANS MONITORED?

Once appointed, guardians acquire enormous power. While most professions with anywhere near this level of power are licensed and supervised by the state, including doctors, therapists, plumbers, and hairstylists, the only two professions in most states that are not licensed or under direct control of the Department of Professional

INVENTORY REPORTS

Guardians are required to document the property they seize from their wards in what are called *inventory reports*. They are required to update these inventories at intervals. These reports are the primary mechanism by which judges are supposed to evaluate the quality of a guardianship, but multiple studies have shown that, in nearly half the cases in certain states around the country, these reports are never filed or are filed very late, thus crippling the ability of even the most upstanding judge to monitor and supervise adequately the guardians they appoint.

Regulation are lawyers and guardians—the two dominant players in the guardianship industry.

Lawyers are presumed to self-police through their state's Supreme Court system of bar regulation. Guardians, however, are subject only to the supervision of the judges that have appointed them and act with near immunity as a result of their status as "court officers." When appropriate, the public has assumed the ability to report guardian malfeasance to various agencies in different states, including the Department of Children and Families, or other similar agencies, such as the Office of Public and Professional Guardians (OPPG) in Florida. This is how the system functions. It fails far more than it should.

Unfortunately, guardians throughout the country are rarely supervised, even more rarely monitored and, even more rarely than that, disciplined or removed. They do not fear loss of licensure because they have no license to lose. As long as they remain in the good graces of the judges that appointed them and keep out of the newspapers and media exposés, they can rely on the fact that those in charge of monitoring and disciplining them will almost always be silent, take their sides in disputes, side with their attorneys, and avoid all but their most flagrant malfeasances.

This ineffective architecture creates an environment that is rife with abuse, neglect, and exploitation. Even though most states have very specific rules, legislation, and administrative offices (like Florida's OPPG) that deal with guardian misconduct, this power is usually applied against family members or family guardians, but rarely against professional or even public guardians. Even when it is used against abusive professional or public guardians, the most that can usually be done to them is administrative sanctioning. Further, most states require that an attorney be appointed to represent a guardian and paid for by the estate of the ward. Supported by this "free" attorney, the guardian becomes almost bulletproof.

HOW ARE GUARDIANS PAID?

Guardians are hourly contractors. Once appointed, they perform their services presumably for the benefit of their wards at hourly rates customarily determined by the courts. These rates vary, but are typically in the range of $70 to $85 per hour for a professional guardian (if a lawyer is appointed guardian, the rate could be $350 to $600 per hour), and slightly less for a public guardian. Typically, a guardian will accumulate a list of charges on a quarterly or semi-annual invoice and submit it to the court for approval, which is nearly always granted with minimal review by a judge.

Like attorneys, these charges are billed in increments of fractions of an hour. For example, a guardian responding to an email might bill at a third of an hour, or twenty minutes, for $28.05. Opening a ward's mail six days a week might be billed at six hours per week or $18,096 per year. A guardian can bill for discussing a case with a social worker, arranging a medical appointment, or just about anything else he chooses. Since guardians can have many wards, even a minimally busy guardian can easily generate $100,000 a year *just for opening the mail* of six wards over the course of a year.

Family guardians are not paid for their services, which is problematic for many. No matter the amount of funds a ward may have, family guardians often must consume much of their own money for the care of their loved one due to family disputes, trust restrictions, or squabbles. These guardians must often abandon their jobs, spend large amounts of time away from their families, and expend enormous amounts of energy on their guardianship duties.

Unfortunately, since family guardianships are the most common type of guardianship by far, it is understandable that critics claim, although wrongly, that they account for the most cases of abuse. It is important to note, however, that families in this situation are usually vigilant and do not hesitate to report any perceived wrongdoings—hence the relatively large numbers of complaints about family guardians.

When the Money Runs Out

It cannot be denied that the primary motivation of professional guardians is getting paid. For their level of education, they are paid extremely well. With the unmonitored ability to tap deep into the assets of the wards for whom they are responsible, with the blessings of the court, estates—even multimillion dollar estates—can be drawn down very quickly, leaving little or no cash with which to pay legal or guardian fees.

At this point, the *modus operandi* of the guardianship system is to sell any and all property owned by a ward as quickly as possible in order to assure that their backdated fees, which have not yet been adjudicated or even submitted, can be covered by the value of the property in question. A guardian will approach a judge for permission to sell a ward's residence, for example, telling the judge it is necessary to do so in order to feed the ward. Many times, however, the goal of this exercise is to create enough ready cash to pay all legal and guardian fees as soon as they are submitted.

Charges are accumulated and summarized in invoices that can be an inch thick and presented to a judge for approval at a fee hearing, which can be closed to the family that is being charged. It is extremely rare for these charges to be effectively opposed or scrutinized by anyone, especially a judge. Typically, these fee requests are rubberstamped, approved, and paid for by the estate of a ward. Neither wards nor their families have any say in the distribution of these fees, which diminish estates repeatedly and substantially.

ARE GUARDIANS BONDED?

Many states require that guardians purchase and maintain *surety bonds* in the event that they incur liability for their actions. The amount of these bonds differs from court to court, and in many cases, the requirement that a specific guardian be bonded may be waived by a friendly judge, ostensibly to reduce the cost of guardianship, but arguably as a professional, though illegal, "courtesy." It would be extremely rare for a bond to be large enough to cover liability from a poorly administered multimillion dollar estate. In essence, these inexpensive, low-level bonds are window dressing.

On the other hand, some bonding can be expensive. In order to serve as a court-appointed family guardian, in addition to the requirement of taking an educational course and fully complying with court-mandated annual reporting, a family member seeking to serve as a guardian must obtain a surety bond in an amount set by the court. The size of the bond may vary, but in many courts it is equal to the total amount of the assets of a ward plus two years' worth of income. The bond's costs and premiums are paid for using the assets of the ward during guardianship.

If a complaint of mismanagement is lodged against a guardian, a hearing may ensue, which the associated bond company's lawyer may attend. This lawyer's fees are paid by the ward's estate. If such an allegation emerges after a guardianship has ended, however, regardless of the outcome of the hearing, the lawyer's fees may then become the personal responsibility of the family member who had been acting as guardian. (Responsibility for such payments is usually tucked away in the fine print of a bond agreement.) This creates another strong disincentive for family members to serve as guardians for loved ones and makes more likely the intrusion of professional guardians.

Can a Guardian Be Sued?

As pointed out, guardians are court officers appointed by a judge whose essentially unlimited judicial immunity extends, at least in part, to those he appoints, including guardians. Consequently it is actually quite difficult to sue a guardian. Assuming a suit is allowed at all, hearings or trials are conducted by the same judge that oversees the guardianship procedure. In addition, the cost of the lawyer hired to defend the guardian being sued is paid for by the ward's estate. The guardian may also take money out of a ward's estate as fees for his time spent on the case outside or inside the courtroom. Therefore, when considering suing a guardian, always take into consideration the legal barriers involved in carrying out a lawsuit, as well as the economic costs that may be incurred by the ward.

The only effective way to take legal action against the guardian begins with local law enforcement. Historically this has been nearly impossible, as law enforcement has been trained to treat complaints against guardians as civil matters requiring attorney litigation, not law enforcement action. A possible exception to this is when hard evidence of embezzlement, theft, or some other felony on the part of a guardian is presented to police or an assistant district attorney.

CONCLUSION

Becoming a guardian can be a very lucrative career choice, and one that requires very little education or training, considering the gravity of controlling another person's entire life. Although most guardians do a good job, sometimes under difficult conditions, the position can attract individuals who cannot resist the temptation to take advantage of the most vulnerable among us.

8

Guardianship Tricks of the Trade

"Given human nature, there's a certain percentage of guardians who will steal. Sometimes they are laypeople, sometimes professionals."
—DAVID ENGLISH, LAW PROFESSOR

There are good guardians, good judges, and good lawyers, to be sure. But, as in every profession, there are some bad apples. Bad guardians exist, as do fraudulent guardianships. David English, a professor of law at the University of Missouri at Columbia, is a knowledgeable expert who has spent decades studying guardianship reform. English has led the drafting of new guardianship laws for the Chicago-based Uniform Law Commission. According to English, studies have found about 10 percent of guardianships involve criminal activity by guardians themselves. AAAPG projects the number of fraudulent or abusive guardianship cases to be around 14 percent of the national total based on statistics from New Mexico alone.

GUARDIAN TRICKERY

There are many common tactics used by unscrupulous guardians to either enrich themselves, their associates, or even their relatives.

And in situations where no traceable compensation is paid out, guardians may be offered favors, provided free services, or wined and dined for their help in bringing in new business. And what business is that? The business of caring for their wards.

Since guardians are paid by the hour and self-report their hours, they can submit invoices in almost any amounts they wish. If guardians are required to travel to see their wards, they expense their travel time. If relatives call to find out how a ward is doing, guardians can charge for their time spent on the phone. If they find themselves in litigation due to a ward's relative trying to stop the guardianship, guardians can charge for the time they spend with their attorneys, in court, traveling, or even thinking about a ward. By simply providing the court with a putative record of time spent performing their guardianship duties, they will be paid by their ward's estate. There are few instances in which hours are checked for accuracy or actual performance of duties. Either you accept the word of a guardian or you don't. And judges routinely do.

A guardian oversees a large amount of a ward's money. Let's say a ward is a widow with no children and has a severe case of dementia. The money is placed into a guardianship account under the sole control of a guardian. The guardian, however, uses these funds for her own personal benefit by fudging the charges. She might charge her ward for all travel expenses, whether they are personal or business. When it is time for her to obtain recertification of guardianship, she might deduct the fee from her ward's funds as a business charge. She might even hire her daughter to do housework at her ward's residence, charging her ward full professional rates at $30 an hour. Unfortunately, this type of behavior is common and clearly against the law. When discovered, it can send a guardian to jail for embezzlement. Due to lack of oversight on the part of the court, however, a guardian is in a position to get away with a very hard-to-detect crime.

A guardian is in a position to hire many service people— from house painters to physical therapists. Over time, working relationships develop. Say one of the service people offers a guardian a cash payment for every client she sends his way. The guardian agrees, and for every job he invoices thanks to her, she makes a percentage. This is very good business for the service provider and the guardian, but it is completely illegal.

The following are more examples of guardian trickery.

Overbilling

As mentioned in the previous chapter, guardians bill by fractions of an hour. If a guardian is required to travel for business to see a ward, she may include her travel time. When a ward's mail is diverted to a guardian, this guardian may charge by the minute for opening and reading it. Guardians may charge for their time spent on mandated visits to wards, going grocery shopping, or appearing in court. If a relative calls to find out how a ward is doing, a guardian may charge for her time spent on the phone call. She may also charge for answering an email or fax or letter. If a guardian finds herself in litigation due to a ward's relative trying to stop a guardianship, she may charge for the time she spent with her attorney and in court.

While these examples may sound reasonable, it is important to understand that, when it comes to guardianships, the only individuals keeping time sheets are the guardians. They have the freedom to log as many hours as they believe they can without raising suspicion. So, if a guardian is a lawyer, she may charge upwards of $300 per hour. By simply providing the court with a record of her time spent performing guardianship duties, she is able to bill her ward's estate with impunity. There are few instances in which hours are checked for accuracy or actual performance of duty. Attorneys who simultaneously act as guardians are prone to bill professional attorney hours for tasks that could easily be done by lower-level individuals. This kind of activity creates massive fees for simple administrative tasks and happens far more often than it should.

Overbilling in the Review of Expense Reports

In many cases, guardians oversee the expenses of other individuals involved in the care of their wards, and these individuals require reimbursement for their services. Receipts for thousands of purchases create a paper trail of money flow and are kept as expense reports and scrutinized by interested parties in requests for reimbursement.

Guardians or their assistants can spend several hours going over expenses. Obviously, this sounds like an important part of making sure a ward is not being overcharged. The problem arises when a guardian spends several hours going over an expense report, finds that a receipt for a $10 charge is missing in connection with the payment for a medication, and then holds up the rest of the expense report process until this receipt is found, even though the credit card bill clearly reflects that the $10 payment was made to a drug store.

For the time the guardian spent reviewing the expense report, as well as the time spent investigating the whereabouts of the missing document, the guardian is able to bill her ward several hundred dollars, all for the sake of a minimal, easily provable expense. And since this review of expenses is recurrent, guardians are able to take advantage of these types of situations without recrimination.

Overbilling in Financial Reviews

A guardian is required to review brokerage investments being held for a ward in a guardianship account. Every few months, guardians meet with financial supervisors overseeing these accounts. When a meeting is held, a guardian can ask her assistant to sit in on it and take notes. After a one- to two-hour meeting, this guardian may bill her ward for both her time and her assistant's time.

Overbilling for Attendance at Court Proceedings

As the procedure of guardianship grinds forward, there may be a number of depositions taken and court hearings requiring the attendance of the guardian. Sending two or even three guardian representatives to simply sit and listen to hours of testimony allows each of these individuals to bill for many hours of court-ordered (and typically unproductive) proceedings.

Charging Corporate Rates While Billing Individuals

An attorney who practices in wills and probate will generally charge one rate for paperwork done in her office, but she may multiply this rate when probate court litigation is involved. Another ploy is to hand off all proceedings to a specialized litigator within the same law office, whose fees are similar to those charged to major corporations for complex business law issues. For a guardian's attorney, it makes no difference because these invoices are almost guaranteed to be paid from a ward's estate when approved by a judge. If a judge approves these high rates, it stands to reason that she will approve the same hourly billing rate for opposing counsel.

Raiding a Guardianship Account

A guardian is required to gather together and oversee a ward's money. This money can be placed in an IRA, a savings account, or a checking account. Guardians are given the authority to write checks from their wards' checking accounts to pay for bills. In some cases, bills must be approved by a judge. In other cases, a guardian is given the right to pay the bill directly as long as a receipt is kept to be handed over to the court. This allows guardians the freedom to be as creative as they can be with their check-writing privileges.

In a situation in which a ward is a widow with no children and has a severe case of dementia, there is little to no oversight in regard to funds spent in the course of caring for her. Experienced guardians can use a number of methods to extract money from guardianship accounts without raising attention.

When a family member or independent observer, such as a banker or broker, becomes aware of the illegal draining of a ward's money, however, law enforcement may be informed and the guardian may be charged with embezzlement. Of all guardianship misdeeds, it is the embezzlement of funds that tends to make headlines.

Embezzlement of Funds

There are endless ways to embezzle estate funds when there is little or no monitoring or supervision of the people that handle these funds. Transfers between accounts, co-mingling of assets, disappearing cash, secretly cashing in life insurance policies, or simply writing checks to one's self are common practices in abusive probate cases. Only the imagination of a guardian limits the number of ways in which she might embezzle funds from her ward.

Free Meals

Receipts for food and dining out to feed a ward may be submitted regularly by a guardian for payment. Many of these bills, however, are expenses incurred not for the benefit of a ward but for food and meals purchased by and for a guardian or other providers. Unless agreed upon in advance, this is clearly a breach of guardian responsibility and duties.

Disappearing Assets

Being in charge of the personal properties of wards provides a number of ways to turn wards' assets into untraceable cash; and as illegal as such behavior is, for the most part, the court system is unable to monitor such transactions effectively. Stories abound of automobiles disappearing in guardianship. When a ward has no family members or family lives out of town, anything in a ward's home that can be removed easily is fair game—from jewelry to antiques to paintings. By failing to list these objects of value on initial and subsequent inventories, no one is the wiser.

Uninventoried Home Assets

In some cases, certain valuable pieces in a home are too big to carry out without drawing attention. By not including these items in an inventory listing, they can be sold off and removed at the appropriate time. Should a family member of a ward notice an item absent from an inventory list, a guardian may provide one of two excuses: If the piece is still there, a guardian may claim it was a simple oversight in recording; if it is gone, a guardian may claim the piece was not there when inventory was taken.

Invisible Properties

In gathering a ward's assets together, a guardian may find properties that may be owned by the estate or in trusts that the court is not aware of. By not reporting these holdings to the court, a guardian can acquire them at her leisure or collect any income derived from them on behalf of her ward—without reporting the revenue.

Profiting from Refunds

A guardian is required to pay many bills on behalf of her ward. By taking advantage of an organization or government agency refund policy, refund payments can result in extra income for a guardian—income that is invisible to the court. For example, requesting a refund on a service and maintenance contract for a major appliance may result in significant cash back, which may then be pocketed by a guardian after it arrives in the mail of a ward.

Life Insurance and Post-Mortem Payments

A ward may have an existing life insurance policy, which, if not paid up in full, can be paid quarterly or annually. By using a guardianship checking account to pay more than the amount requested, a guardian can trigger a refund for the overpayment in the name of the ward. The guardian can then cash the check.

More importantly, it is not unheard of for a guardian to drain a ward's life insurance policy. This can be done by forging the originator's signature on the policy or by using the authority as guardian to trigger insurance payouts to cover guardianship charges when a final fee request is made.

In many cases, since a guardian controls funeral matters as well as the sometimes unannounced information about the death of a ward, she has primary control of and first access to the death certificate. She can even prevent family members from seeing it or getting copies of it in a timely manner. Until a family can procure copies of the death certificate, it cannot provide legal evidence of death of a ward to the insurance company in order to claim the benefits intended for its members. Nor can a family determine cause of death, which at least would provide some closure.

Only a guardian can prove the legal death of a ward to the insurance company and claim the benefits for herself. This is made possible, in part, because a guardian has a ward's mail redirected to her. No one will ever see the insurance payout that comes in the mail or is electronically deposited in a guardian's private account. Whether income taxes or any other taxes are ever paid on this money is unknown.

A similar situation may transpire with any delayed refunds, such as tax refunds, which may appear after a guardianship has been closed and tax reporting has been completed. It is to a guardian's benefit to delay requests for refunds of any type until after guardianship has ended and payments may go directly to her.

Health Insurance

Guardians can pay doctors or medical providers in full with a ward's cash while knowing that a refund will be coming their way because the insured has third-party coverage. The guardian then pockets the refund.

IRS Scam

Each year, guardians are required to have their wards' taxes completed and mailed in, with payments if necessary. Manipulating a ward's income tax returns can result in an IRS refund, which comes in the form of a debit card. A guardian can then use this card for personal purchases.

Social Security, Pension, and Veteran Payments

Guardians may apply for social security on behalf of their wards. They may also legally keep up to 30 percent of a ward's monthly social security, Veterans Affairs, or other pension benefits. These guardians would still control the remaining 70 percent as well.

Finding New Sources of Payment

At a certain point in a guardianship, a ward's disposable cash may run out. All the bonds and stocks have been sold off and the guardianship bank account is empty. At this time, bills must be covered by non-cash assets, such as a ward's home, investment properties, or inventoried assets that may be converted into cash. For many guardians, selling these assets quickly allows them many inventive opportunities to enrich themselves.

Lowball Sales

Because any real estate holdings of a ward must be sold quickly, appraisers may be found to lowball the value of these properties—establishing prices below their actual values. An appraisal document for a property is given to a judge for approval, and then this property may be sold to a guardian's attorney or associate within twenty-four to forty-eight hours. In turn, this same property may be sold at its full price to an outside buyer.

When a ward's inventory has been recorded and cannot be taken out without notice, the same lowball appraisal technique may be used. A valuable item may be appraised at a price of almost nothing and quickly purchased by an associate of a guardian. The piece is then sold at a higher price to an antique shop or to one of the guardian's associates in the business.

Letting a House Fall Apart

The maintenance of any home can be costly. From leaks in the roof to bug infestations to boilers that stop working, the list goes on. In some instances, as time goes by, the house slowly falls under disrepair because the guardian does nothing to maintain it. At a certain point, the house is declared condemned.

If a ward is living in a nursing home facility while his wife is living at home, she will be forced out of the home upon its condemnation. As a condemned home, it can be listed as almost worthless and purchased by a guardian's associate for very little. At this point, the guardian does all the repairs, charging the work to her ward. The newly renovated house can now be resold at full price.

The Foreclosure Gambit

When a guardian withholds tax payments on a ward's property, this property can be taken over by the county through a foreclosure procedure. Once the property has been foreclosed on, it will be sold off through a county land sales auction. Many times the property is offered at a price equal to its past-due taxes or slightly higher. At this point, a guardian or a guardian's colleague buys it at a below-value price, only to resell it later at a higher price. Since all mail may be forwarded directly to a guardian, any past-due tax notices or foreclosure documents sent to a ward may be deliberately ignored by a guardian until the house goes into default.

Estate Sales

Upon the death of a ward, when there are no relatives, a guardian may sell all the inventoried property of a ward in order to settle any outstanding invoices. For the work involved in selling a ward's properties, a guardian may bill a deceased ward's estate and keep the money from the sale.

Medication Management

When wards complain too much about the conditions they are forced to endure, guardians can make arrangements with complicit doctors to medicate these wards with psychotropic drugs. These drugs are designed to impair their cognitive abilities—putting the wards into trance-like states to the point that they can do little else but what they are told. Many of these psychotropic drugs have dangerous side effects. These pharmaceuticals are very helpful, especially when given prior to hearings to silence wards, or to keep senior wards from disturbing anyone once they have been placed in homes. Of course, one nasty side effect is that it turns functioning seniors into zombies within a day or two.

In addition, guardians can be paid handsomely by pharmaceutical companies to enroll an unsuspecting ward in a clinical drug trial as a test subject, especially for psychotropic medications.

Every Vote Counts

The right to vote is a precious United States civil right guaranteed by the Bill of Rights. But in the event that someone is deemed totally incapacitated, it is likely that she will not be allowed to vote according to her personal preferences again. The right to vote can be removed from a new ward. A guardian, however, can cast a vote for any of her wards without even knowing their preferences. Some guardians insist that their wards retain the right to vote. In this situation, a guardian may vote for the candidate of her choice on behalf of her ward. This power may turn lucrative when judicial elections come around. When a guardian is in charge of a significant number of wards, it is not unusual to see all of them vote for the same candidate.

Paying for Leads

A guardian's lifeline is referrals for new wards. Guardians can pay for leads from investigators at the Department of Children and Families, who are the first line of inquiry when a complaint is made about a vulnerable adult. Leads can also come from nurses or social workers, especially those in hospitals, rehab centers, or nursing homes.

CONCLUSION

Becoming a guardian is a rather simple procedure for those so inclined, and the requirements are often minimal for a position of such tremendous power. The selection and approval processes are unhindered by significant barriers to certification, and there is no licensure process. It is even easier to remain a guardian. Oversight and discipline over guardians is almost nonexistent. The result is that guardians who have assumed complete control of another vulnerable person are free to act with relative impunity as long as they are covered by the umbrella of court immunity extended by friendly judges.

The average American would have no reason to be familiar with this situation or with how many times it occurs. Only a person who has been personally involved in the process can begin to understand—or even believe—the abuses that occur in guardianship on a daily basis in nearly every state in the country. Sadly, with the greying of America, guardianships are bound to increase in number, as will the abuses associated with them.

9

The Lawyers & Probate Activities

"It is the trade of lawyers to question everything, yield nothing, and talk by the hour."
—THOMAS JEFFERSON

Guardianship legal fees are often the single biggest drain on a ward's estate. While a guardian might be paid as much as $85 per hour (or as much as $350 to $600 per hour if a guardian is also a lawyer), a guardian's attorney, who is paid exclusively from the estate, may charge hourly fees that are hundreds more than this amount. Moreover, it is not uncommon for multiple attorneys of varying degrees of seniority, paralegals, legal assistants, or other members of a law firm's staff on either side of the issue to bill concurrently. Over the course of years of litigation, which is not an unheard of length of duration in regard to contested involuntary guardianship cases, these fees can reach into the multiple millions.

Guardianships are often ignited and spurred on by disagreements among family members. Litigators representing all sides can take full advantage of these situations and may even intentionally stoke the flames of discord, all for the one thing that drives them: legal fees. Guardians are able to hire the best, most expensive lawyers to defend themselves because their legal bills are paid by the estate of their wards. In other words, a ward is forced to pay a guardian's lawyer to litigate against family members or anyone else who might object to any aspect of the guardianship. Anyone who wishes to challenge a guardianship must pay his own legal fees.

Lawyers in this field work primarily in probate courts. It is important to understand the responsibilities of the probate equity court and how this court affects individuals and their assets both during guardianship and after death.

WHAT IS PROBATE?

Probate is the court-based administrative process of distributing the assets of a person who is deceased. This function is typically non-adversarial, except in unusual cases. A person who dies *intestate*—meaning without express instructions in a legal document on how to distribute his solely owned assets—will have the payment of his bills and distribution of his remaining assets adjudicated by an administrative judge in a probate equity court.

This part of what happens in probate court is not particularly complex, controversial, or adversarial; it is routine business. But the amount of money passing through probate on a yearly basis across the country is enormous, in the trillions of dollars yearly, so there is a tremendous amount at stake in these proceedings. This simple reality, and the billing opportunities it creates, has given rise to two entire subclasses of attorneys who specialize in probate court matters: Real Property, Probate, and Trust Law (RPPTL) and Elder Law.

Both groups of attorneys are very active politically and have substantial influence and impact on the creation of probate legislation, and particularly on the creation of probate rules. They figure prominently in the official nomination process, election, and reelection of probate judges, and members of each group are frequently substantial donors to their campaigns. Members of both groups often have wide and deep social connections and belong to the same religious organizations and charitable groups, country clubs, or special interest groups. Their spouses often interact with one another, as do their children.

Real Property, Probate, and Trust Law Attorneys

Attorneys belonging to the Real Property, Probate, and Trust Law sections of their state bar frequently appear in guardianship cases. RPPTL attorneys have practiced and have an interest in real property (including construction), probate, trust, or related fields of law. According to Matt Leichter, author of the *Law School Tuition Bubble* blog, of the over 105,000 attorneys in Florida, 59,400 are employed and active, and 11,000 are members of the RPPTL.

These attorneys specialize in creating plans and documents that have, among other things, the express purpose of avoiding taxes on the distributable assets of an individual, thereby safeguarding the inheritance plans of a *testator*, which refers to a person who hires this type of attorney to make these plans. In addition to their activities in probate court, you can find these attorneys involved in litigation or other legal activities regarding construction—in particular, condominium development.

Elder Law Attorneys

Elder law attorneys advocate for the elderly and their loved ones. They handle a range of legal matters that affect older and disabled people, including the following issues:

- Advanced directives, including wills, powers of attorney, estate arrangements, and other forms of long-term planning.

- Healthcare, including long-term care options, patient rights, Medicare, and arranging healthcare powers of attorney.

- Financial representation, including financial planning, income, estates, and gift tax matters.

- Locating long-term care facilities and managing the cost of assisted living.

- Explaining nursing home resident rights and how to file nursing home claims.

- Guardianship, including the selection and appointment of a legal guardian.

WHAT ARE PROBATE RULES?

Probate attorneys are governed by applicable statutes and, in many states, an additional layer of administration called *probate rules*. These rules are agreed upon and written by large committees of attorneys from the two primary groups mentioned at the outset of this chapter. Probate rules determine what is and what is not adversarial, and provide guidance concerning countless other issues that only insider lawyers (and judges) would recognize. They are extremely complex, lengthy, and occasionally incompatible with statutes.

Amazingly, statutes are superseded by probate rules whenever there is a conflict. Florida probate rules indicate that Rules of Civil Procedure, as in civil cases, should apply in all cases—except where they say they should not! For example, attorneys in non-probate, civil, or even criminal cases have only thirty days to file their fees with the court. Probate rules exempt attorneys from this general rule of civil procedure and give them latitude to withhold bills for an indefinite period of time. This convenient exception allows probate attorneys to delay filing their requests with the court until late in the process, when most people are fed up with it and are more likely to settle.

WHICH ASSETS GO THROUGH PROBATE?

Not all assets will go through probate in the event of death. Primarily, the assets that will be probated are those with a title in the deceased's name, such as bank accounts, investments, homes, vehicles, etc. Probate court alone has the power to replace the deceased's name on a title with someone else's name.

Assets that typically do not go through probate are either jointly owned and go to the surviving owner, have a valid beneficiary designation, or are in a trust. This is not to say, however, that such assets always avoid probate.

Jointly Owned Assets

Jointly owned assets skip probate and are transferred to the surviving owner in a situation known as "joint ownership with right of survivorship." This shift in ownership occurs immediately after the death of the first proprietor, even if his will indicates that the assets in question should go to someone else in the family, such as a son or daughter. The surviving proprietor will gain possession of the assets, essentially disinheriting the deceased's children. In the event that a surviving owner dies without designating another proprietor, or both owners die at the same time, the assets must go through probate before they can be passed on to the rightful heirs.

A second type of ownership is known as "tenants-in-common." In this kind of ownership, the assets are distributed as directed in the deceased's will and will not go to the other proprietor unless the will indicates as such. This allows the deceased a bit more control over who will rightfully inherit their belongings, but the assets will still have to go through probate.

Beneficiary Designations

Certain assets, such as insurance policies, retirement plans, or even bank accounts, can theoretically bypass probate altogether and be paid directly to a person of the deceased's choosing in his *beneficiary designation*. There are a few scenarios, however, in which this is not the case. These include the following:

- If a beneficiary dies before or at the same time as the original owner, the proceeds will go through probate and be distributed with the rest of the deceased's assets.

- If a beneficiary is a minor or incapacitated, probate court will appoint a guardian to take control of the assets.

- If a beneficiary is listed as an "estate," the assets will go through probate and be allocated along with the rest of the deceased's possessions.

Living Trusts

Assets that are written into a *living trust* as opposed to a will avoid probate. Living trusts are similar to wills in that both indicate how a person known as a *grantor* wishes his assets to be distributed after his death.

The biggest difference between living trusts and wills is that a will goes into effect only after a grantor has died and his will has gone through probate. A living trust, on the other hand, allows a grantor to designate an individual to become his successor trustee in the event that he is determined incapacitated. A trustee takes control of a grantor's affairs in place of a guardian. Living trusts bypass probate in favor of a trustee, who is responsible for carrying out a grantor's instructions and desires as documented in the trust.

A trust documented in a person's will is known as a *testamentary trust.* This type of trust must go through probate along with the rest of a will in order to become effective.

Trust Invasion

The invasion of trusts is a major point of contention in the guardianship process and litigation. Frequently, an aggressive litigator will attempt to break a trust to remove it from the security of assets that are protected until after a ward has died into assets that are available to be tapped during the lifetime of a ward while in guardianship. Often, these formerly protected trust assets are used to pay legal fees for the benefit of a guardian's attorney. With a bit of legal wrangling, an attorney may create not only fees for himself but also the ability to have these fees paid in full from assets that were specifically designed not to be touched until after the death of the ward. These fees are often paid in full with very little investigation or oversight by the court.

UNIQUE PROBLEMS WITH LAWYERS IN GUARDIANSHIPS

Finding a lawyer to represent you in guardianship court is often very complicated. When anger, guilt, and fear are the primary drivers of an urgent need to have representation in a guardianship matter, rational analysis can be hard to achieve and decision-making becomes that much more difficult. Accusations of being an evildoer by opposing counsel can foster lawyer selection based on emotion rather than analysis of his credentials or success rate. Even in an ideal scenario, there is no perfect method to ensure the right choices are being made.

When it comes to finding representation, many start out by seeking out the top practitioners in their field, but they may not be available to you. Especially in smaller court districts, there are only a limited number of expert guardianship lawyers to choose from, all of them likely court insiders. Their services are in high demand by their fellow insiders.

Consequently, each of the really good attorneys who have had success in probate court has likely worked for and represented many, if not all of the other court insiders. This creates what is known as a *conflict of interest* for the attorney in question, which will prevent him from working in any case against any of the court insiders involved in your case. The result of the situation is that litigants in guardianship courts are forced to choose from second- or third-tier lawyers who have little experience and even less success for their clients involved in guardianship litigation. This is just one of several significant disadvantages for a first-time guardianship litigant.

Another major disadvantage to guardianship litigants is that lawyers are never placed under oath in front of a judge. They are free to say or allege whatever they want and will never be called out for doing so. But in probate courts, where a judge chooses "good guys" and "bad guys," lying becomes a weapon of mass destruction. Worse yet, one of the most common complaints from victims is that even after years of hearings, not once did they or their counsel have a viable opportunity to respond to the salacious lies meant to portray them as evildoers.

Commonly, guardianship family litigants change lawyers when the results they were promised by their first attorneys are not forthcoming. This further reduces the number of available attorneys while increasing the cost of litigation, since each new attorney must start from scratch on every case. With each change of attorney, the likelihood of success is diminished and approaches zero when the only option left for family members who have no further funds is *pro se* representation.

Litigation in guardianships is extremely expensive. Few families can afford the enormous legal fees involved in protracted guardianship litigation, which can take years to resolve. Complicating this matter further is the reality that contingency fee agreements in probate litigation are almost never available.

Contingency fee agreements involve an arrangement in which an attorney and client share the risk of the outcome of the case. Attorneys are loath to involve themselves in contingency fee cases they know have a very small chance of success, and therefore little chance of generating recovery fees. Within the legal community, it appears to be a well-known reality that going head-to-head in court with one of its insider attorneys is a losing proposition. This is one reason why hourly fee arrangements are usually the only options available to guardianship litigants, and why it is so common for families to spend their entire life savings embroiled in endless and typically pointless guardianship litigation.

Guardianship litigation is a bruising battle. Guardianship disputes are highly contentious. Accusations and allegations divide families and often cause irreparable damage to lifelong relationships within families. Lawyers involved in these battles are trained and highly incentivized to win at all costs, no matter what. In a legal system with endless twists and turns, litigants are easily overwhelmed by the amount of paper and pleadings generated, the legal tricks executed, the speed or lack thereof in these proceedings, the frustration of never seeming to be able to win, and the seemingly pointless and endless billable hours. Battle fatigue is an almost universal reality that grinds down everyone but court insiders, and it is often the burden of legal fees that become the most powerful weapon and punishment in these contested guardianship proceedings.

Clinical manifestations of this protracted form of battle have been labeled as "legal abuse syndrome" by Dr. Karin Huffer and include both physical and psychological damage.

Sovereign Immunity Issues

Guardianship cases can be worth millions in legal and guardian fees and wealth extraction. But the ability to take legal action against rulings that might be proven to be inappropriate or just wrong is severely limited by not only judicial immunity but also by dollar caps placed on any (extremely rare) successful suits against the state itself. Ultimately, the state is responsible for the actions of the Supreme Court and all lower courts.

Currently, in Florida, there is a cap of $200,000 on any proceeds from a successful lawsuit against the state, although such a case might have caused millions in damages to the plaintiffs. There is, however, an arcane, seldom-used process called "claims bills," which, in theory, allows greater recoveries by lifting the cap through the passage of a sponsored legislative bill requesting relief. Unfortunately, this technique has been banned from time to time— the legislature does not like giving money to claimants—and many times claims bills languish for years before they either die or are withdrawn. The system is again tilted in favor of court insiders who have judicial immunity, an almost foolproof shield against lawsuits. In the event there is any recovery in a lawsuit, it is realistically limited to $200,000 by sovereign immunity.

CONCLUSION

Litigation is highly profitable for guardianship insiders because it creates enormous fee profits without risk to guardians or the lawyers who defend them, judges, or anyone else in the guardianship system. Although there are really never any winners in guardianship litigation, wards seem always to be the losers in probate court, and are often referred to as such by insiders.

Both types of lawyers that regularly practice in probate court are highly organized and sophisticated. In addition to their experience and skill sets, they have the advantage of long-standing relationships with probate judges and staff. They also benefit from judicial immunity. Their everyday presence in probate court versus the occasional appearance of a non-probate insider attorney tilts the playing field even more decidedly in favor of these insiders.

Even a lawyer representing the interests of a ward or ward's family, intentionally or not, profits enormously from an insider's ability to create dissent and, in particular, protracted litigation over every petty detail of a case. A ward's family finds itself at an enormous disadvantage when it attempts to do what it thinks is right in a system that is rigged from start to finish.

10

The Estate Liquidators

*"Say not that you know another entirely
until you have divided an inheritance with him."*
—JOHANN KASPAR LAVATER, SWISS POET AND PHILOSOPHER

When all is said and done, soon after a ward is dead, litigation dies down a bit and the time comes to figure out what (if anything) is left of the estate. A new group of hired hands enters the picture, selectively chosen by a guardian to help facilitate the liquidation of a ward's estate. But as we will see, the primary motivation of these court insiders remains the same: to do everything to ensure all fees will be paid from the estate.

Over a lifetime, a person can collect a lot of stuff. When the life of a ward is over, this stuff needs to be disposed of—a task that would normally be performed by inheritors and family but now falls to a guardian. Most guardians do not have the background or education to place valuations on property, or the time or interest to dispose of it. The most effortless mechanism to liquidate an estate as quickly as possible is to call in an estate liquidator, who does all the work for a hefty fee.

According to the American Society of Estate Liquidators, estate liquidation "is an industry laden with pop-ups and fly-by-night companies, many of which have no principles and may be using questionable practices. . . ." It should not be surprising that kickbacks and rigged fees for this terminal service "in the best interests of the dead ward" occur.

WHAT HAPPENS TO THE ESTATE OF A DECEASED WARD?

Whatever property remains in an estate must ultimately be disposed of. Whether the property is worthless or priceless, it must be moved. Sentimental property, such as photographs, heirlooms, or remembrances, is worthless to a guardian, but this does not mean it has no value to a ward's family. It is not unusual for a guardian to extract money from family members who wish to retain items precious to them. Since family dysfunction is a major reason why guardianships occur in the first place, a guardian can take advantage of animosity between family members by having them bid against one another to purchase items that they normally would have inherited anyway for free.

A guardian benefits from this exploitation of a ward's family, as money raised from family members will almost certainly not go to the heirs but rather used first and foremost for the payment of guardian and legal fees. Guardians are all too willing to set up competitive bidding among family members (who have already been at each other's throats for a long time) for the purchase of sentimental items, threatening to destroy these items if they are not sold.

In the meantime, larger items, like furniture, must be moved to a storage facility at a price that can exceed the total value of the items stored. They are ultimately donated, divided, or discarded. Any remaining valuables, like art or jewelry, must be reappraised so they can be distributed. If there is real property that has fallen into default, then it must be put up for sale. Any back taxes or liens must be resolved. If there are claims against the estate, they must be adjudicated. Seeing to these matters takes a lot of work, which is paid for by the estate, of course.

ESTATE LIQUIDATION OPTIONS

A guardian's duties technically end shortly after the death of a ward, but she is still responsible for ensuring that all outstanding debts are paid in full—including legal fees, and of course, her own accumulated and ongoing charges. To address these post-death issues, a guardian transfers her responsibility to liquidate an estate to a court-appointed curator, accountants, charities, movers and storage facilities, funeral directors, and many others—all of whom have their hands out to the guardian, who still controls all the money.

The Curator

At the top of the food chain is a court-appointed curator, who is left to handle a deceased ward's affairs once a guardian's responsibilities have ended. Remaining debts could easily exceed the value of an estate. In Florida, statutes guarantee curators 3 percent of the estate. Additionally, the longer a curator is in charge, the more hourly fees she can bill. Since a curator is typically an attorney, these fees can be as high as $800 per hour, which is why curators never seem to work fast—doing so is not in their economic interest.

Accountants

Especially in large estates with trusts and real property, accountants play a central role in preparing documents for the government to collect whatever taxes are due from an estate before it closes. This can take years. Families are typically not included, nor are their interests a concern in the process, so preparation of tax returns to benefit an estate may do the opposite for its heirs, possibly even exposing them to fines and penalties.

Large accounting firms are in the habit of using multiple members of their team, from the most junior to the most senior, to prepare estate tax documents, all billing at different levels, with senior accountants getting up to $400 per hour. Bills are rarely scrutinized by the court and are paid before any funds are available to heirs. They are always paid from the funds of the estate under the assumption that the work they do benefits the ward. After the death of a ward, accountants' fees are a major source of wealth extraction from the estate. Once the accounting work is complete and they are paid for, however, whatever IRS issues might remain become the problem of the heirs.

Movers and Storage Facilities

Movers and storage facilities love doing work for guardians. While families often do this type of work themselves or hire cost-efficient movers to clean out the home of a deceased ward, curators, who have little or no incentives to save money for estates, often hire nationally known, expensive, heavily insured moving companies to clean out the residences of deceased wards. Every item is treated as though it is priceless, driving costs up. These things, often unwanted by anyone, are packed and moved to storage facilities, but because of family disputes, cannot be distributed in a fair fashion. So they remain unused, gathering dust or rusting in storage facilities until decisions can be hammered out about their ultimate disposition. These storage facilities can run from $200 to $1,000 per month. That which is left after everything of value is picked over and removed must be disposed of. If a municipal trash collection service doesn't accept certain items as refuse, then more money ends up being spent on a private trash hauler.

Funeral Directors

Funeral directors receive a lot of business from court insiders, since they control the final arrangements of many wards whose only way out of guardianship is death. Statutes require guardians to make funeral arrangements but allow guardians the discretion to turn this responsibility over to the families. But when a case becomes very contentious, and a guardian chooses to take one last shot at retaliation against a family, dropping this responsibility in the hands of the family can be a particularly brutal move at a time when everyone is upset and vulnerable.

Conversely, funeral directors have been known to assist in preventing families from attending the services of loved ones, bringing security guards to the cemetery to prevent entry of family. In one hotly contested case, an actual email sent from a guardian to the daughters of a ward on the day of the funeral stated, "Please be advised that they have a strict NO GUNS or other weapons allowed policy at the cemetery. If you bring any type of weapon with you, you will be escorted from the premises." The family in question did not own guns or threaten violence, but was terrified to attend the funeral.

ESTATE LIQUIDATION OPTIONS

There are a number of simple, tried-and-true estate liquidation options available. Normally, outside of guardianship, the decision about which method to use would be at the discretion of those in line to inherit. In guardianship, assets in an estate may not have the same importance or value to a guardian, so expediency rules the day.

Assets must be liquidated and turned into cash (to assure adequate monies to pay fees) quickly—although there are exceptions to this rule. For example, when family members of probate insiders own secondhand or antique stores, where assets from a ward's estate sometimes mysteriously show up, the "donation" of certain items to the business by a guardian can bring handsome profits, with no time limits for a sale.

Under normal circumstances, the object of estate liquidation is to maximize the proceeds of an estate for the benefit of heirs. Upon the death of a ward, however, fees accumulated over the course of guardianship may exceed the value of an estate. Expediency dictates that the assets be disposed of as quickly as possible, even if this means not getting anywhere near their true net value.

Consignment and Charity Shops

Consignment sales are a somewhat effortless option for a guardian in a hurry to offload items from an estate. Consignment is essentially asking a third party to sell items at its storefront or weekend sale. In return for its services, the third party receives a percentage of each item sold. There are two types of consignment arrangements: brick-and-mortar stores and limited consignment sales.

Consignment storefronts carry higher quality big-ticket or interesting items, such as leather furniture, buffets, small collectables, or precious metals. Limited space and low inventory turnover makes consignment stores very picky. Items consigned are usually given a maximum of ninety days to sell, with a large price reduction every couple of weeks until they are sold or taken back by the guardian. Consignment sales, on the other hand, are typically two- to four-days long and run in churches, school gymnasiums, civic centers, or any building with a large, open area.

Charities and resale shops, especially those that a guardian or curator favors—or might possibly own—often receive "donations" of a ward's possessions for resale to the public. Of course, these donations are never reflected on the ultimate tax return of the ward. In one infamous case, the charity turned out to be the very probate judge who created the ward's involuntary guardianship. This fact was discovered when she was seen in public wearing an expensive, one-of-a-kind piece of jewelry custom-made for the ward.

Online Auctions and Estate Sales

Online auctions have been around for quite a while, with the most common being eBay. Online estate sales begin by hiring a company to evaluate the contents of a home (at the expense of the estate) to decide if there are any items of value. Then the company will place pictures and descriptions of each chosen item on its website. As items are sold, they are shipped off to their respective buyers, who are usually responsible for shipping costs.

FEES AND COSTS
AFTER A GUARDIANSHIP HAS BEEN ESTABLISHED

Once a guardianship has been established by the court, many of the ongoing duties and responsibilities of the guardian will require payment—from the estate of the ward—of certain fees and costs. These may include the following:

- **Attorney fees for a guardian.** In many instances, a guardian will be required to seek court approval before taking specific actions or making certain decisions on behalf of a ward. This, in turn, will lead to fees for the preparation and filing of the appropriate court petition, plus the costs and fees associated with any hearings required by the guardianship judge.

- **Attorney fees for a ward's attorney.** If a judge requires a guardian to have a court hearing for any reason, then the ward's attorney will need to attend the hearing and be paid for doing so.

- **Accounting fees.** Each and every year, a guardian is required to file an accounting of how a ward's assets have been bought, sold, invested, and spent on behalf of the ward during the previous year. A guardian may need to prepare this report himself, hire and pay an accountant to prepare it, or pay his attorney to prepare it.

- **Court fees.** Depending upon state law, court fees will be incurred when a judge requires a hearing and when the annual accounting is filed with the court.

And all these issues come up before a dollar of care, medicine, shelter, clothing, food, or protection has been rendered.

The Most Significant Cost of Guardianship

Of course, these initial and ongoing monetary fees and costs do not represent the most significant cost incurred due to a court-ordered guardianship. The most significant cost has nothing to do with money. Instead, it is the emotional cost of the complete loss of control experienced by both a ward and a ward's family. But guardianship is a for-profit business, and business is business, right?

THE GUARDIANSHIP BUSINESS

The day-to-day business of a guardian includes major decisions about money management. But the goals and principles of this money management are very different than those of the person who accumulated this money in the first place. More often than not, the value of an estate declines precipitously during guardianship, especially in fraudulent guardianships. There is increasingly little to manage, since legal and guardianship fees constantly drain accounts and absolutely destroy any concept of reinvesting dividends or interest, while major chunks of principal are diverted into the hands of court insiders on a regular basis.

Getting Professional Help for Guardians

Guardians, especially those with many wards in their books of business, reach out for help in these situations. With their vast powers, and with a judge's consent and approval, every scrap of estates with monetary value is seized, put under court-order, and frozen—especially funds that are in banks or financial services accounts, such as those handled by a financial adviser.

This typically precipitates the first crisis in a new guardianship: when cash on hand runs out and there are no funds available to family to pay for a ward's ongoing needs or prior financial obligations. It may take weeks or even months for arrangements to be made to deliver cash on a regular basis to caregivers for the maintenance of a ward.

For a ward, being forced to depend on only cash in modern America is a cruel anachronism. With no credit cards, no checks, and no source of currency other than deliveries of just enough to get by on from a guardian (based on a budget submitted to the court—which never includes legal or guardian fees), a ward and his caretakers are placed into the untenable position of paying for everything with cash, and therefore carrying around large amounts of it. Anyone carrying large quantities of cash becomes a potential target of violence and injury, which further complicates the already difficult task of caring for an elderly person.

INVENTORY MANIPULATION

One of the challenges of creating an inventory for a judge's review and approval is that objects of value that are not cash or equities must be appraised, which is often a difficult task. For example, a ward's diamond ring must be appraised to place a certain value on it for the inventory.

Appraisers

Enter the appraiser. Most financially minded individuals know that there are a number of ways to create valid appraisals of non-monetary assets such as jewelry. The best appraisal of an object of value from a guardian's perspective is a *low-ball appraisal.* This is often called "current" or "resale" value. Manipulating the value of a ward's non-monetary assets by low-balling their initial values for inventory purposes allows these items to be sold for far less than their real values dictate. A guardian is subsequently able to profit from the immediate resale of these items. Similarly, appraisers have a large role to play in real estate evaluations as well. The same holds for sales of used cars or furniture, which may be sold when cash runs out.

Banks

The number of people and institutions draining assets in guardianships is stupefying. Banks, however, profit enormously from the deposition of funds from guardians into their institutions. These funds are placed in non-interest-bearing accounts, which are the absolute best accounts for banks, as their costs and fees generate the most money for them. Banks often assign cash or fund managers to manage this money—and pay these managers significant fees to do so. Since guardians routinely close credit card accounts, and cash is the preferred medium of exchange for purchases for wards, frequent service trips to banks become a necessity. Issuance of large amounts of cash with little or no record kept opens the door to all kinds of shenanigans with other people's money.

Brokers

A brokerage account created by a guardian with a ward's money is prone to abuse as well. Since guardians do not monitor these accounts, nor do courts, brokers are known to take advantage of the situation by creating excessive numbers of transactions and fees, which they pocket. A broker may also choose to invest a ward's money in riskier financial vehicles than the ward might ever have chosen.

Accountants

Accountants play a large role in guardianship. Forensic accountants are often hired to theoretically prove the presence of financial abuse against an elder for huge consulting fees and billed hours. They are also responsible for completing tax forms and tax filings for a ward in guardianship. Their fees are uniformly accepted without question by the court. If there are tax issues, accountants can run up bills for hundreds of thousands of dollars to do research on tax opinions in regard to estate tax obligations or problems. Guardians do not routinely report certain expenses, such as medical expenses, to accountants. Therefore, certain tax deductions are not routinely applied to the tax returns of wards, thus increasing their tax burdens.

Thorny Tax Issues

There are also serious questions about whether the fees charged by guardians and taken from their wards must be reported as income on the income tax filings of guardians. This is a complex matter, but there are strong voices that suggest guardians often break the law by not reporting the money they have accrued from wards as income. These omissions result in lost revenue for state and federal governments.

STRAW MAN SALES

Time and again, guardianships generate "straw man sales" through real estate transactions. The system works this way: When a ward's cash assets eventually run out, the guardian approaches the judge to say that these funds are almost gone, and suggests raising money by selling the ward's home. The story told to the judge is that unless the property is sold and soon, there will be no money left to care for the ward, but the guardian's true motivation might simply be to get paid before everything is gone. The judge may then request, for the sake of propriety, an independent appraisal to be done.

Enter our friend the appraiser, who, for a fat fee, is happy to undervalue the property in question. This appraisal is brought to the court, which authorizes a sale at a fraction of the property's true value. It is generally sold to a colleague of the guardian, most commonly his attorney, for a bargain-basement price. This sale is reported to the judge.

Within a short amount of time, the buyer is able to flip the house and sell it at full market value, pocketing the profit in what we call a "straw man sale." This profit is never reported to the judge, who believes that the money collected from the first sale is the only way to take care of the ward's dwindling finances. In fact, the proceeds from the first sale are typically used to pay past-due or existing guardian or legal fees rather than care for the ward.

What About Material Possessions?

Similar situations exist with antique stores, secondhand stores, estate sales, jewelry stores, and used-car salesmen, all of whom work with guardians on a regular basis to dispose of any items of lesser value, no matter how little of these transactions go into wards' accounts. The tactic is always the same: Convince a judge that something has little or no value, obtain permission to dispose of it, appraise it with a low-ball estimate, and sell it to a friendly vendor after telling the judge that it was worthless. Profit follows. As for sentimental items with great personal value that cannot be adequately estimated, these items are typically thrown away or offered for competitive bidding to family members.

POST-MORTEM MONEY MANAGEMENT

Guardianships theoretically end with the death of a ward. But even though a ward is dead, his money still exists and must be eventually distributed after all outstanding obligations and fees have been paid. A curator is a personal representative that takes over the responsibility of managing a ward's estate after his death and the exit of his guardian. Since this exit may take a long time and guardians are notorious for filing paperwork late, a curator will often assume responsibility for the money immediately after a ward's demise. His job is to make sure the money does not disappear and is eventually distributed to the appropriate heirs as per a deceased ward's estate plan.

What Is the Role of a Curator?

As mentioned in the last chapter, curators get paid by the hour and work closely with bankers and other financial institutions. Curators are usually lawyers who charge high-end fees. Often, they take years to distribute whatever funds are left, and there are frequently heavy-duty legal battles about inheritances that delay their distribution and enrich curators. In the end, after being drained by so many individuals for such a long time, families are often shocked to see multimillion-dollar inheritances vanish.

CONCLUSION

The money that enters into the control of professional guardians was accumulated over a lifetime. It was likely intended to support its originator for the remainder of his life. It was certainly never intended to feed the insatiable monetary appetites of an army of wealth extractors brought in by the guardianship system with the blessings of the court. It becomes sadly apparent that these funds are not being managed in the best interests of wards, but are being methodically siphoned from estates by a ravenous system of wealth extraction that all begins with an unproven allegation that an individual is in need of a guardian.

12

The Caregivers

*"Caring for our seniors is perhaps
the greatest responsibility we have.
Those who walked before us have given so much
and made possible the life we all enjoy."*
—JOHN HOEVEN,
UNITED STATES SENATOR FROM NORTH DAKOTA

The large caseload presented to favored guardians by judges makes these guardians very busy people, even though they are not expected to render in-person services or care for their wards. In fact, many guardians do not visit their wards more than two or three times a year, if at all. Instead, they hire others to do the day-to-day work of taking care of these protected individuals. The people who actually do the hands-on tasks involved in caring for a ward are referred to as "caregivers."

Prior to guardianship initiation, if caregivers for a loved one were needed, one would either be drawn from relatives or hired by the ward or other family members at their discretion. The number of hours per day and the amount of compensation given would be up to the family. If services were not rendered appropriately or there were problems with the caregiver, the family member in charge would be able to fire and replace her with someone more appropriate. In other words, there would be a spoken or written contract between the parties.

All of this changes in guardianship.

WHO ARE THE CAREGIVERS?

Guardians need to develop close relationships with the agencies that hire individuals as caregivers. Dealing with one caregiver at a time is not efficient. Even if a caregiver has been with a senior for years, once guardianship begins, he is typically replaced or forced to join an agency favored by the guardian. Although he will be providing the same level of service, it will now be at a marked-up price. Caregiver agencies manage low-level helpers, hiring them out to provide costly, non-negotiable around-the-clock care, whether needed or not. This service offers cover to a guardian in the event that an adverse situation takes place during what would normally be off-hours.

It is common for a ward to be provided with one or more certified nursing assistants (CNAs) around-the-clock at the first blush of guardianship. Often, a ward has been previously cared for over a long period without difficulty, typically by a registered visiting nurse, which is paid for by Medicare or other insurance. A guardian's rationale may be that more care at more cost results in less exposure to problems, especially to unforeseen circumstances such as illnesses or accidents.

How Much Are Personal Caregivers Paid?

A guardian will frequently choose to employ twenty-four-hour-a-day caregivers for a ward, stating that doing so is "in the best interests of the ward." Home care agencies are paid top dollar by guardians using their wards' money. For example, the national average hourly salary for a CNA is about $15 per hour. Agencies ratchet this amount up to about $22 per hour in many places, covering their administrative costs and profit margins. Cost of direct care for a ward then goes from seven days a week, eight hours a day at $15 per hour—amounting to $43,800 per year—for one full-time CNA, to seven days a week, twenty-four hours a day at $22 per hour—resulting in a cost of $192,720 per year, with much of this billable time referring to when the ward is sleeping and requires little care.

All of this is not only non-negotiable but not even discussed with the family of a ward, and, in fact, occurs over any family objections. Worse still, guardians employ CNAs as informants to report any unwanted visitation attempts or interference from family. Of course, the home health and nursing agencies also bill Medicare or any other available insurance for registered nurses and physical therapy visits, adding more to their profit margins.

Professional Caregivers

A ward may have a perfectly satisfactory, long-term relationship with a physician or clinic, but it can be ended in guardianship. Choice of doctors and facilities for a ward are at the sole discretion of a guardian. All the headaches involved in switching medical care providers come into play, including transfer of medical records and introduction of new specialists and new facilities. In facilities or clinics where a doctor might see dozens of patients in a day with whom they have little familiarity, wards are prone to experience errors, mistakes, or overmedication, which could have been avoided if they had remained under the care of a familiar provider. Making matters worse, wards are routinely overmedicated by anonymous prescribers, who indiscriminately use controller drugs to keep them quiet, intentionally or by indifference to their well-being. Pharmacies that do business with guardians are given a stable profit stream, which increases with every new prescription.

Home physical therapy, paid for by Medicare, is another way for an agency that deals with wards to profit from unneeded or excessive home visits that have little or no benefit to the ward. DME (Durable Medical Equipment) suppliers have ready-made recipients for their oxygen units or other supplies needed for frail patients, including beds, commodes, and canes—all paid for by Medicare.

Medical transportation costs are prominent features of guardianships. What used to be a courtesy ride to the doctor provided by a family member, neighbor, or friend becomes a very expensive ambulance trip, which not only costs hundreds of dollars but also takes far more time, is very public, and is far less comfortable.

The results of replacing professional providers for the convenience of a guardian are often inferior care, dangerous medical practices, and poor health outcomes for the ward. Further, by exhausting estate funds needlessly and excessively, a ward that might have had enough money to last a lifetime becomes impoverished and ends up on public assistance at taxpayer expense.

Caretakers

Caretakers watch over property and offer emotional support to those in need. Every property owner understands that properties constantly need attention, even if the property is simply an empty lot. An owner with a vested interest in a property takes care to maintain it so that it may be utilized or sold at a decent price in the future.

For court insiders, maintenance of property of a ward is a very low priority. Instead, their primary concern is to assure that the property benefits guardians when it is time for fees to be paid. In fact, it is usually in a guardian's best interest to let a property fall into disrepair, which would convince a judge that it must be sold expeditiously before it loses any further value. Of course, the reason for this eagerness is to ensure payment of legal or guardian fees, which may be paid using proceeds from the sale.

There have been instances in which a guardian is faced with the problem of a ward's spouse maintaining residence on the couple's property. In order to remove this spouse from the home, the guardian, who has total control of the property, delays necessary repairs to the house until she is able to report it as uninhabitable (not fixing a leaky roof, for example). The spouse is then ousted from his home, shortly after which repairs are made. The newly renovated house is put on the market in good condition, ready for a quick sale and the extraction of more estate funds to pay accumulated legal or guardian fees.

Emotional Caretakers

Emotional and psychological caretakers are often a ward's friends, neighbors, co-parishioners, or acquaintances—the people who help weave the fabric of our daily lives. When family may be less than accommodating, good friends and neighbors enrich our lives and keep us going. They are available when we need them to comfort us and vice versa, and over the years these relationships give us fulfillment and purpose. When a ward is isolated from friends and neighbors, as is so often the case, or when she is suddenly and unexpectedly removed from her home, she loses important connections to the real world and suffers as a result. The pain to all concerned is very real. The wounds that result never heal.

CONCLUSION

The consequences of bad guardianships may be measured in dollars and pain. Perfectly adequate care that had been more than efficient prior to guardianship is regularly made excessive, the primary goal of which is not the welfare of a ward but the generation of profits, monetary or otherwise, for multiple, guardian-hired, downstream service providers. Guardianship can more than quadruple the cost of routine care, which is extracted from a ward's estate and redirected out of the hands of legitimate heirs and into the profit margins of guardianship insiders and their allies. The psychological life of a ward can also be irrevocably damaged by the actions of a guardian, who may be more concerned about convenience and profit than with the emotional well-being of her ward.

13

The Abridgment of a Ward's Rights & Advance Directives

"We wouldn't have to take your rights away if you'd just stop exercising them."
—CARL-JOHN X VERAJA, WRITER

O ur entire American legal system hinges on the faith and trust of the American citizen. When faith and trust in the system are challenged, our country suffers. Our country's three foundational government documents—the Declaration of Independence, the Constitution and its Amendments, and the Bill of Rights—take great pains to enumerate and guarantee the unique ideals that countless Americans have been willing to die for. Our tacit understanding with government is that if we abide by the laws of the land, our sacred rights will be guaranteed. Only if we break the laws of the land would we be subject to incarceration and the loss of these rights.

In guardianship, however, everything is different. Innocent individuals can be stripped of their rights by probate courts. It is almost as if being incapacitated is no less of a crime than being a serial murderer. In fact, most wards have even fewer rights than do convicted serial murderers.

141

The foundation upon which the guardianship process rests is the idea that certain people in our society, whom courts label as "incapacitated," must have their rights removed for their own protection and the protection of others. These wards need help to be safe, it is thought, and this help and protection should come from government benevolence carried out by court-appointed guardians. This seems to be appropriate, enlightened, and compassionate reasoning. Unfortunately, guardianship interventions are often not benevolent.

Even after an individual has been deemed incapacitated, a guardianship need not necessarily be created. Rather than follow the statutes of just about every state, which state that guardianship should be the very last choice for an incapacitated person, and that a less restrictive option is always preferred in connection with such an individual, probate judges around the country almost automatically rule to impose guardianship in cases of incapacitation.

It is important to note that every incapacitated person is covered by the Americans with Disabilities Act, which is routinely violated when the civil rights of seniors are stripped away in guardianship courts. The United Nations weighed in with its support of the rights of the disabled in 2006, when it adopted the Convention on the Rights of Persons with Disabilities and its Optional Protocol at its New York headquarters. The convention was the first comprehensive human rights treaty of the twenty-first century. In terms of people with disabilities, including incapacity, it views them not as objects in need of charity and protection but as subjects with rights who are capable of making their own decisions as active members of society. Unfortunately, in spite of this convention, American courts continue to consider guardianship as the first option instead of the last.

RIGHTS IN GUARDIANSHIP

According to the Florida Guardianship Association, whose guidelines are widely imitated and echoed in nearly every state, state laws prohibit the removal of the following basic civil rights of a ward:

- To be represented by an attorney.
- To have access to a court.
- To receive a proper education.
- To be free from abuse, neglect, and exploitation.
- To remain as independent as possible.
- To receive necessary services and rehabilitation.
- To be treated humanely, with dignity and respect.

Certain basic civil rights, however, may be removed by a guardianship court during or even before a determination of incapacity has been reached, including the right to:

- travel.
- vote.
- marry.
- petition for dissolution of marriage.
- consent to termination of parental rights.
- decide on living arrangements.
- manage money and property.
- apply for a driver's license.
- seek or retain employment.
- apply for governmental services.
- sue and defend lawsuits.
- consent to sterilization or abortion.
- consent to medical, dental, surgical, or mental health treatment.
- commit a person to a facility or institution without formal placement proceedings.

Without these basic rights, and under the complete control of the court system, an individual who has committed no offense other than to age in America becomes a non-person. Probate court, which deals with the assets of dead people, makes a ward "dead" in terms of the law, stripped of the rights that America promised the ward in return for the obligations of citizenship, a mere piece of property owned by a court insider.

For those who are not at all or only minimally incapacitated, the realities of the world of guardianship can send them and their families into despair. Anxiety, fear, depression, and physical symptoms like heart disturbances, metabolic issues, and sleep problems can arise and become very hard to treat. In addition, few people know that probate courts have and use the authority to sterilize incapacitated individuals. Although the risk of this happening to an elderly ward is not very high, incapacity determinations are being made in connection with younger and younger individuals, who could still be in their childbearing years.

ADVANCE HEALTHCARE DIRECTIVES

An *advance healthcare directive,* also known as a living will, personal directive, advance directive, medical directive, or advance decision, refers to a collection of approved documents through which a person specifies the actions that should be taken for his benefit or health if he becomes no longer able to make decisions for himself because of illness or incapacity.

These are formal documents intentionally designed to prevent guardianship, spurred on by the rapid advancement of medical technology, which can artificially keep a patient alive with little or no quality of life. Additionally, the evolution of the hospice concept has underscored the need for individuals to make known their wishes for the way they would prefer to be treated at the end of life and how they would like their financial affairs to be handled. The promise of advance directives is that an individual's wishes will be carried out if he is unable to make decisions for himself.

The Five Wishes

Although there are many resources when it comes to creating advance directives, the organization Aging with Dignity, based in Tallahassee, Florida, offers an online method of creating a legal set of advance directives that will be acceptable in nearly every state, featuring an excellent framework called "five wishes." This easy-to-understand process, designed primarily for seniors, allows the user to address the following wishes for his future care:

Wish 1: The Person I Want to Make Care Decisions for Me When I Can't

Wish 2: The Kind of Medical Treatment I Want or Don't Want

Wish 3: How Comfortable I Want to Be

Wish 4: How I Want People to Treat Me

Wish 5: What I Want My Loved Ones to Know

The widespread acceptance of the concept of advance directives has been swift. Today you cannot check into a hospital or even an emergency room without being asked if you have advance directives. Most doctors' offices and almost every other type of medical facility will inquire and recommend that you complete a set of advance directives to have on file. The unspoken promise of advance directives is that you will have the opportunity to decide, long before the day when this decision is critical, how you wish to be treated in the event that you cannot decide for yourself, and to express your choices despite incapacity of any sort, whether temporary or permanent.

NULLIFICATION OF ADVANCE DIRECTIVES

The nullification of a ward's advance directives is a very serious matter. It pulls the rug out from under even the most carefully constructed end-of-life wishes. Doing so has a dramatic impact on families, caregivers, and, of course, the individual. According to reports documented in guardianship abuse surveys by Americans Against Abusive Probate Guardianship, probate judges across the country have shown a propensity to ignore their statutorily-mandated obligation to adhere to advance directives, thus effectively removing the single greatest barrier to the creation of a guardianship.

Advance directives, often prepared by probate lawyers, are generally intended to prevent probate. They are the main tool available to average citizens to state their wishes about who will take care of them and who will run their estates, should they become incapacitated. The first and most serious act that initiates an abusive probate guardianship is a probate judge ignoring, failing to recognize, or nullifying advance directives, or in any way preventing advance directives from being executed.

Once advance directives have been nullified, probate judges can open the door to guardianship, court-appointed lawyers, and litigation. Litigation immediately and massively profits insiders at the expense of the very person the court is meant to protect. The assets of wards are used to pay court fees, clerk fees, and filing fees, not to mention fees for guardians and all the people guardians may hire.

Dissipation of a ward's assets becomes almost a certainty. The impact of this one decision sends ripples throughout not only the family of a ward but also society. Once a ward has become destitute, his assets having been consumed by guardian and legal fees, it is the state—you and I—that will bear the burden of his medical care, housing, food, and clothing through programs like Medicaid, which suffers regularly from deficits.

HOW ARE ADVANCE DIRECTIVES NULLIFIED?

There are a number of ways a court can prevent the execution of a ward's advance directives. Procedurally, the existence of advance directives must be formally presented to a court for them to be considered. There may be difficulties finding them, but commonly, insiders simply fail or forget to inform the court that advance directives exist. If advance directives are presented at all, it is not until after guardianship has been instituted, which effectively nullifies their execution.

Additionally, even when presented with valid advance directives, probate judges sometimes claim that these directives were created improperly because the individual in question may have been incapacitated at the time they were produced, thereby nullifying them. Ignored is the fact that any attorney who creates advance directives for an incapacitated person is committing serious legal malpractice.

Nevertheless, this malevolent judicial tactic has led to countless cases of fraudulent guardianship. It is nearly impossible to prove that a person was capacitated at a given time in the past once they have been ruled currently incapacitated. Similarly, if advance directives do not contain clear-cut prohibitions against the appointment of a professional guardian, a judge may interpret this omission as permission and consent to proceed with the appointment of a professional guardian.

Another trick is to disqualify any individual identified in advance directives as a potential guardian by accusing him of various troublesome acts, including influencing the creation of the advance directives in question. Typically, the person selected to become the guardian in case of need is the person closest to the ward, likely his primary caretaker. Assassinating the character of this individual removes him from consideration, eliminating another barrier to fraudulent guardianship.

Can Nullification of Advance Directives Be Prevented?

Although not guaranteed or foolproof, the following tactics may be used to create stronger, "next level" advance directives and reduce the likelihood of their nullification:

1. Rather than naming a single individual as your potential guardian in your advance directives, create a list of individuals who would be acceptable to function in this role, whether these individuals are family members or not. The list should include at least six names. It would be very difficult for a judge to disqualify that many people, and although the last choice on your list might be far from your first choice, it is a better choice than a stranger.

2. Create a video that demonstrates the basic elements of capacity at a given point in time and simultaneously records your wishes for end-of-life care. Include evidence of your capacity by providing your knowledge of location, time, person, and place; the names of your family members; current issues, such as the names of the last two or three presidents; the location of your assets; and the names of your medical caregivers.

3. Be sure that the location of your advance directives and video are well-known to family members. Make copies and distribute them so there will be no questions about where they are or what they contain. Include your attorney and physician in this distribution list.

4. Include current contact information for your family members so there is no excuse to say they could not be reached for notification from the court.

5. Create a baseline Medical Certificate of Capacity, notarize it, and update it regularly. This medical document is designed for a medical professional (ideally, a mental health or neuroscience specialist) to certify that an individual is fully capacitated at a given date in time. This will tend to defeat allegations that advance directives were prepared by an incapacitated individual.

6. Demand that any lawyer or law firm you hire to create these documents also agrees, in writing, to defend them if challenged.

Too often lawyers determine that it is not in their firm's interest to defend the very directives you have paid them to create, opening a trap door to guardianship.

Note that there is no guarantee that any medical certificate of capacity will be accepted or honored by any probate court.

ALTERNATIVES TO GUARDIANSHIPS

Many lawyers go on and on about how durable their documents are in regard to power of attorney and healthcare proxy, but these documents often fail to protect individuals from guardianship in judicial hotspots. Even after taking all the precautions recommended earlier, ultimately a judge can always create a guardianship if he so chooses, for almost any reason. This is why avoidance of guardianship altogether is the best way to retain your rights later in life if you end up needing some degree of help. Our society must find better ways to offer help to those who need it.

While national guardianship incidence is rising, some experts feel there is a growing paradigm shift from punitive, court-controlled guardianship—referred to as *substituted decision-making*—to a more rights-focused, less intrusive option that is being championed by leaders in the disability rights community: *supported decision-making*. A movement encouraging the use of supported decision-making, or SDM, more frequently than substituted decision-making has begun in response to the troubling issues surrounding substituted decision-making and the glaring need to provide a less invasive alternative to traditional guardianship.

Supported decision-making allows an individual with a disability to work with an advisory team of his choosing and make personal choices about his own life. Under this model, an individual creates his own trusted support network to aid in decision-making, as opposed to the guardianship-industrial model, in which a court and its officers impose a paid network of professionals on a ward.

SDM promotes self-determination, control, and autonomy. It fosters independence. Unlike substituted decision-making, in which guardians, family members, or caregivers make decisions for an individual, supported decision-making enables a person to make his own decisions with assistance from a trusted designated network of willing supporters. In this scheme, a person in need of help or protection can reach out to family or trusted friends for advice on everyday or special life decisions before he makes them. After consultation, decisions may be reached and executed.

Members of these unpaid volunteer personal networks may be family members, co-workers, friends, or providers who have personal relationships with these "protected" people, know their preferences, and will honor the choices and decisions they make.

Why Is Supported Decision-Making So Important?

Demographics, especially regarding baby boomers, are clear. There will be a lot more people in need of help and protection over the next few decades, and many believe the current guardianship system is no longer an acceptable mechanism to care for these emerging cases.

For millions of existing wards in America, guardianship has forced them to experience a kind of "civil death," as they have no rights to make their own decisions about their personal healthcare, finances, associations, or other day-to-day matters the rest of us take for granted. Data suggest that by the year 2030, there will be several million intellectually disabled individuals over sixty years old in the United States, who will all be at risk of guardianship.

Although it is only now gaining a foothold in the United States (Texas recently became the first state to pass SDM legislation), supported decision-making has been evolving in other countries for more than a decade. Several countries have long held that everyone—including individuals with disabilities—has legal capacity. This holding was further advanced when the United Nations Convention on the Rights of People with Disabilities voted in 2006 to adopt Article 12, which states that "persons with disabilities enjoy legal capacity on an equal basis with others in all aspects of life" and that "[all] parties shall take appropriate measures to provide access by persons with disabilities to the support they may require in exercising their legal capacity."

CONCLUSION

Since the founding of our country, millions have died protecting our cherished rights when they have been threatened. Our civil rights may be the most precious and important elements of our lives as Americans. Taking these rights away should be incredibly difficult, and occur only under exceptional circumstances. People accused of criminality, for example, are innocent until proven guilty. Our legal system goes to great lengths to provide incontrovertible proof of serious wrongdoing before the constitutional rights of an accused person are taken away. We even provide free access to public defenders for the accused. Why do we not afford potential wards the same level of treatment received by alleged criminals?

Rights can vanish in a heartbeat—and in secret—in probate court hotspots across America. Doing everything possible to protect these rights should be among the highest priorities of any individual, particularly seniors and their loved ones. We must find a better approach to the inevitable decline that accompanies aging, one that strengthens our rights instead of stripping them away.

14

Guardianship Abuse & Its Consequences

*"What I fear most is power with impunity.
I fear abuse of power and the power to abuse."*
—Isabel Allende, writer

The progression of guardianship has been described as "litigate, isolate, medicate, and take the estate." This description encapsulates how the industry, under the nose of the court, exerts its will over those it controls, extracting the wealth and health of its victims through abuse of the system and its wards.

Guardianship abuse can take a number of forms. These types of abuse arise from a lack of oversight and discipline in the guardianship process, particularly in relation to the guardians and lawyers in the system. Guardianship abuse is rooted in the misuse of power by an individual who is in a position of authority over another individual who is in a vulnerable and helpless position. It seems practically self-fulfilling.

RECOGNIZING ABUSE

To understand abuse, you must be able to recognize it. Some of the hallmarks of an abusive guardianship include the following:

- The victim's family members have visitation restrictions.

- The victim is not given adequate exercise.

- The victim is not fed well and is losing weight.

- The victim is covered in bruises but her facility denies trauma.

- The victim is in a locked-down unit and medicated with powerful antipsychotics with no evidence of a psychiatric diagnosis.

- The victim is on multiple antipsychotic, pain, and sleeping medications.

- The court-appointed guardian does not give accounting of funds taken from the victim.

- Large sums of the victim's funds are missing.

- The victim's home is sold below market value for quick sale.

- The court prohibits family members from telling press or media what is happening.

- The victim appears to be zombielike from psychotropic drugs.

- The victim is left with only the right to vote. This vote may be used by the guardian.

- The victim's money is used to sue her own family members by the court-appointed guardian.

- The victim's trust, will, and durable power of attorney are nullified by the court.

- The family and friends of the victim are harassed, threatened, or intimidated by authorities.

- The family and friends of the victim are charged with "custodial interference" if they try to help their loved one.

For a professional guardian who has been awarded dozens or even hundreds of wards by the same judge or judges and gets away with abuse time after time, it is very easy to understand that this guardian will not hesitate to victimize her next ward in the same way. It is the temptation of easy money and power that motivates guardians and pushes them to do anything and everything they can to continue their profitable business ventures, even if doing so means inflicting grave harm on innocent people.

DEFINING ABUSE

The Centers for Disease Control and Prevention define *elder abuse* as the intentional act, or failure to act, by a caregiver or another person in a relationship established on the basis of trust that causes or creates risk of harm to an elderly adult, or someone aged sixty or older.

Forms of elderly abuse include:

- financial abuse or exploitation.

- emotional or psychological abuse.

- physical abuse.

- sexual abuse or abusive sexual contact.

- neglect.

Other forms of abuse include misusing an elderly person's checks, credit cards, or bank accounts; stealing cash, income checks, or household goods; forging an elderly person's signature; engaging in theft of an elderly person's identity; perpetrating scams, including telling an elderly person she has won a prize but must pay money in order to claim it, or getting an elderly person to donate money to a phony charity; and investment fraud.

Many advocates refer to the totality of these abuses as *elder human trafficking*. The major difference between garden-variety human trafficking, whether for labor or sex, and elder human trafficking, is that trafficked laborers and sex workers produce money on a daily basis by virtue of their work. This money is then improperly taken from them by the traffickers. In elder human trafficking, the money has already been earned and saved. It is easily located in the process of marshaling all the assets of a ward and readily available at the stroke of a judge's pen.

But there may be reason for hope. In 2017, President Trump signed an executive order declaring a national state emergency in human trafficking, including elder trafficking, which may have far-reaching impacts on abusive guardianship going forward.

NURSING HOME ABUSE

Already vulnerable elderly wards are most at risk of abuse when they become utterly dependent on nursing home care, especially when orchestrated by a greed-driven guardianship system. Wards with physical infirmities or dementia are low-hanging fruit for unscrupulous guardians, nursing home owners, and especially low-level, poorly trained, and desensitized staff.

Greed often plays a substantial role in elder abuse in nursing homes, especially when guardians collude with facility owners. Motivated by profit, many nursing home owners employ caregivers who are poorly trained, or hire people without first conducting adequate background checks (in some cases employing people with histories of abusive behavior). Convenience plays a role for guardians, too—it is very easy to have all their wards in one place, where they can easily be managed with little effort.

Being a ward of an uncaring guardian—especially in a nursing home, where you are at the additional mercy of whatever staff is assigned to you—exposes you to a litany of easy-to-identify dangers, including:

- unnecessary physical restraint resulting in debilitation.

- physical or sexual abuse.

- lack of or substandard medical care.

- welts, wounds, or injuries (e.g., bruises, lacerations, dental problems, head injuries, broken bones, pressure sores, infections).

- persistent physical pain or soreness.

- slip-and-fall accidents leading to fractures.

- nutrition or hydration issues.

- sleep disturbances.

- increased susceptibility to new illnesses (including sexually transmitted diseases).

- exacerbation of preexisting health conditions.

- increased risk of premature death.

- high levels of distress and depression.

- increased risk of developing fear and anxiety.

- feelings of helplessness.

- post-traumatic stress disorder (PTSD).

According to Susan Mitchell, geriatrics professor at Harvard Medical School, residents of for-profit nursing homes, where so many wards may be found, are much more likely to have feeding tubes. (See "Feeding Tubes" on page 159.) She says nursing homes may exploit reimbursement rules that allow them to charge higher rates for "high acuity" patients in need of specialized treatment. There is also the added bonus that tube-fed patients are actually less expensive to care for and require less interaction with nursing staff than would hand-fed patients. "If you get paid less, but require more staffing, it is hard to make the case for hand feeding," Dr. Mitchell said. Perverse financial incentives like this one are rampant in guardianship.

The excessive use of feeding tubes is linked to another major abuse in guardianship—namely, the use of chemical restraints, also known as the excessive or improper administration of psychotropic drugs. According to a study published in 2009 by Dr. Victor Molinari from the University of South Florida, researchers determined within three months of admission, 71 percent of Medicaid residents in Florida nursing homes were receiving a psychoactive medication, such as an antidepressant, antipsychotic, or dementia drug, but had not been given psychiatric diagnoses. In addition, 15 percent of residents were taking four or more such medications, while only 12 percent were getting non-drug treatments such as behavioral therapy.

Overmedication of the elderly is a scenario that is repeated every day in nursing homes all over the country, and one that is encouraged by the pharmaceutical industry. In fact, in 2010, the Department of Justice brought criminal charges against Eli Lilly and Company, accusing this large pharmaceutical firm of illegally marketing its antipsychotic drug Zyprexa to doctors who were working in nursing homes and assisted living facilities, encouraging them to prescribe it for sleep disorders and dementia. It has been approved, however, only to treat schizophrenia and bipolar disorder. The company agreed to pay $1.4 billion in a related civil settlement.

The indiscriminate administration of high dosages and combinations of antipsychotic medications, tranquilizers, narcotics, and sleeping pills—employed as "handler drugs" (drugs to subdue and silence disruptive patients)—to the elderly can lead to an array of complications, including constipation, nausea, and imbalance. But the most damaging side effect is anorexia, or the inability or lack of desire to eat. In the elderly, the immediate consequence is serious dehydration and its resultant problems, including malnutrition. This lack of calories takes a devastating toll on bones and muscles.

Rather than tapering or discontinuing the use of these drugs, however, nursing homes frequently resort to the use of feeding tubes, yet again, to keep wards alive. The glaring nutritional deficiencies are thus "solved," avoiding scrutiny, discipline, or fines from supervisory agencies—and as a benefit, saving money for the facilities, as staff needs to spend little or no time feeding the wards or caring for them. This situation explains why so many elderly individuals in nursing homes can be found lying or sitting in their own excretions, covered in bedsores.

FEEDING TUBES

Forced feeding is a particularly horrific medical assault on wards, and it may be the most perverse of all. Bedridden or debilitated wards often cannot access water or other liquids on their own. Keeping a debilitated ward well-hydrated takes constant attention. Absent this attention to keep patients properly hydrated, wards weaken, making them even more hopelessly vulnerable to the infections so pervasive in nursing home environments.

Dr. Haider Javed Warraich, a fellow in cardiovascular medicine at Duke University Medical Center, wrote about the issues with tube feeding in the *New York Times*. According to Dr. Warraich, millions of elderly Americans, many of them wards, are fed through tubes despite a lack of substantial evidence pointing to any clinical benefit of this system. Intended to provide nutrition for patients—increasingly, patients with dementia—who are unable to eat on their own, tube feeding is a troubling and dire intervention for helpless wards as they approach end of life and develop difficulties in swallowing. Inserting a feeding tube through the nose into the stomach is very painful. If prescribed for long-term use, an invasive procedure is performed with anesthesia to place a plastic or silicone feeding tube through a hole in the abdomen directly into the stomach. Often multiple interventions are needed to keep the tube from blocking up. Tubes can easily become infected as well.

Studies have repeatedly shown that tube feeding does not provide any benefit compared with feeding these patients by hand, which is more labor-intensive and expensive for residential facility owners but much better for the patients. Tube feeding has never been shown to have a significant benefit in such cases. Instead, tube feeding is associated with disadvantages such as pressure ulcers, prolonged immobilization, and tubes becoming clogged.

Pressure to place feeding tubes comes from various sources, such as the patients' family, physicians, or facility owners. Often, it is guardians who insist on this invasion for their convenience. Feeding tubes do not improve patient quality of life, morbidity, mortality, or survival rates. A growing number of physicians firmly believe they should not ever be used in patients with dementia of any kind.

Of course, other medications, including antibiotics and vitamins, may be needed and supplied at a hefty mark-up to treat the complications of being in a stupor, which was caused by the first round of drugs. The entire sad and pathetic situation is a bonanza for the pharmaceutical industry and everyone associated with it.

Other abuses happen in nursing homes, which are all too often the final worldly destination for wards who should have been allowed to remain in their homes but for the need to sell their homes to pay guardianship bills. According to the Centers for Disease Control (CDC), each year in the United States there are more than a half a million reported cases of elder abuse. Because thousands of cases go undiscovered and unreported, the actual number is considerably higher. While elder abuse in nursing homes is pandemic, there are also plenty of cases of abuse that occur at home.

HOSPICE ABUSE

A ward might have been stripped of her rights, her estate, her home, and her family, but even her last few remaining breaths can bring big profits to industry stakeholders and colleagues by putting her in hospice. Since being authorized in 1982, the Medicare hospice benefit has grown steadily. Over one million Americans are in hospice today, creating Medicare payouts to vendors of over $13 billion annually.

As Medicare payments for hospice care continue to soar, a sadly familiar and predictable pattern of fraud, excessive billing, inappropriate enrollment, and other devious tactics has emerged, as have a variety of illicit schemes to obtain hospice benefit payments improperly. Billions are available to unscrupulous predators in the hospice business, who may collude with unscrupulous predators in the guardianship business. Since hospice care is more profitable, wards may be found in hospice when they are not at all near death. A person in hospice, however, receives a different kind of medical care than someone in a nursing home—mainly narcotics or psychotropic medications intended to treat pain while she awaits death. Other treatments for things like heart failure are not used, as the patient is considered terminal. Many hospice patients, who might be wards, do not die within the expected six-month period, however, and remain a source of profit for many months. And since communication with family members is not a responsibility of the typical guardian, families are sometimes shocked to learn that a loved one has been in hospice for quite a while.

ISOLATION OF THE ELDERLY

Elders often suffer indignities as they age and slowly lose certain abilities. One complication of aging is the loss of friends, family, and associates. This gradual shrinking of one's social circle is a primary driver of elderly isolation and a serious challenge to the welfare of seniors. Isolation is well known to have adverse effects on health.

The removal of an elderly person from a stable, loving environment to an unfamiliar, possibly unfriendly one is a grievous blow. Forcible isolation and denial of access to loved ones are seldom recognized but devastating traumas that affect all aspects of an elderly person's well-being. Yet they occur routinely in guardianship.

The stress and abuse heaped on vulnerable seniors in guardianship is shocking. When a ward is isolated and then put on powerful psychotropic medications to neutralize the emotions that accompany isolation, what follows is the destruction of a human being.

Despite clear legislative intent to minimize guardianship-generated isolation of the elderly, most states have been slow to recognize the magnitude of this disastrous problem. In some states, including California, isolation of the elderly has been added to the legal definition of elder abuse, and violations of this prohibition carry significant penalties. But most state statutes fall short of the California standard and do not specifically refer to isolation as a serious issue worthy of being called elder abuse. Without a precise directive from legislatures, and with little or no oversight in the guardianship process, especially in plenary guardianship, an abusive guardian can lord over the ruin of her ward.

Guardianship-related isolation may be viewed on a spectrum. Naturally, individuals who are violent or otherwise uncontrollable may require occasional seclusion for their own protection and the protection of others. But the vast majority of cases of court-ordered isolation of the elderly are the direct result of the guardianship apparatus wanting to exert absolute control over an individual and her assets, even when it is not necessary to isolate her.

Isolating a ward is a potent weapon. The anguish it causes is disarming and may force a family to capitulate to a guardian in its battle to save a loved one—only to find this capitulation being used against them when a judge hears that the family "agreed" to a particular action of the guardian.

Isolation Greatly Reduces Cognitive Skills

In "A Review of Social Isolation," published in the June 2012 issue of *Journal of Primary Prevention*, Dr. Nicholas R. Nicholson examines the condition of isolation, which is usually underdiagnosed despite a wealth of evidence regarding its harmful outcomes. He explains that social isolation negatively impacts health in multiple ways.

Isolated seniors, who are without the positive influence of a social network, are at an elevated risk of engaging in many negative behaviors, such as heavy drinking, smoking, and being sedentary. They also experience increased nutritional risk. By not participating in leisure activities, isolated seniors are more likely to experience rapid cognitive decline. Men, in particular, are at a significantly increased risk of death from suicide, as well as from other causes. Dr. Nicholson posits that isolated wards are at increased risk for all manners of morbidity and mortality from falls, repeated hospitalization, and institutionalization. Social isolation is also a strong predictor of mortality from coronary heart disease and stroke.

RELIGIOUS ABUSE

Other forms of ward abuse are subtler. For example, limiting the movement of a ward will also prevent her from attending religious services. Feeding a ward food that is not in accordance with religious dietary laws is cheaper than observing those laws. Observing religious holidays can be impossible unless a guardian not only consents to same but also assists in their observance by instructing caretakers to provide the help needed to prepare sacred rituals, such as the Jewish Sabbath observance with candle lighting, sacramental wine or juice, and traditional challah bread for blessing. When old lives do not matter, though, these things are unimportant.

As briefly mentioned in Chapter 10, a guardian's disregard for her ward's religious wishes can continue even after the death of the ward. For example, certain religions prohibit the performance of autopsies (post-mortem examinations) on their adherents. Since there is no requirement on a guardian to notify family members of a ward's death, wards are routinely subjected to autopsies regardless of their religious beliefs in life. As well, guardians often make unilateral decisions about funeral arrangements without considering the religious wishes of their wards. Cremation is the method of choice for guardians typically, but cremation is absolutely forbidden in several religions. The cremation of a ward frequently comes as a shock to her family members, who, upon finding out about it, can do nothing.

TAX ABUSE

Many guardianship companies are set up as 501(c)(3) corporations, meaning that they are not-for-profit organizations, which can accept donations as such. This implies that the work they do is for the public good. Many questions have been raised in regard to the tax responsibilities of guardians and their wards. For example, there is the question of how and when income tax reports are filed

RIGHTS OF A WARD

The laws of most states enumerate the residual rights of a ward. They generally include the following rights:

- To have an annual review of the guardianship report and plan.

- To have continuing review of the need for restriction of rights.

- To be restored to capacity at the earliest possible time.

- To be treated humanely, with dignity and respect, and to be protected against abuse, neglect, and exploitation.

- To have a qualified guardian.

- To remain as independent as possible, including having her preferences as to place and standard of living honored, either as she expressed or demonstrated prior to the determination of her incapacity, or as she currently expresses, insofar as such requests are reasonable.

- To be properly educated.

- To receive prudent financial management of her property and to be informed how her property is being managed if she has lost the right to manage property.

- To receive services and rehabilitation necessary to maximize quality of life.

- To be free from discrimination due to her incapacity.

- To have access to the courts.

- To have access to counsel.

- To receive visitors and communicate with others.

- To maintain privacy.

These residual rights of a ward, like all other rights, require enforcement to be of value and achieve their intended purposes. It is the responsibility of government, and especially law enforcement, to protect these and all other rights. Sadly, this simply does not happen often enough.

by guardians for their wards, and of whether all available deductions are being taken to minimize their ward's tax burdens. It is not at all unusual for guardians to file tax returns late and incur penalties, which are eventually paid by their wards' estates. Tax deductions for legitimate expenses, including medical expenses and fees charged by guardianship, never seem to make it onto a ward's tax return.

In addition, as noted in Chapter 11, court-approved fees and proceeds from the sale of property collected by a guardianship are not generally reported as income by a guardian on her own corporate or personal tax return, an omission that likely violates the law. Of course, none of this ever comes up because guardians' taxes are not generally subject to investigation.

As mentioned in Chapter 8, guardians may legally keep up to 30 percent of a ward's monthly social security, Veterans Affairs, or other pension benefits as representative payees. Most will not list this source of income on their tax returns. Although these guardians avoid paying any taxes on this income, estates are still held responsible to pay taxes on social security benefits paid. When AAAPG confronted the Social Security Administration with this fraudulent activity, the agency replied by stating that, while it was aware such activity was occurring, little could be done about it.

LEGAL ABUSE SYNDROME

An abusive guardianship process affects more than just the ward. Being forced to endure a never-ending barrage of lies, character assassination, adversarial depositions, and legal bills, as well as the disappearance of retirement funds, is a profoundly awful experience for wards and their families. The average guardianship lasts for years and is typically full of stress and legal abuse for the families involved.

Just the stress that comes with choosing and dealing with *your own attorney* can be maddening. Most attorneys, even second-tier attorneys, will demand a pricey retainer for even considering your

VIGILANCE OF FAMILIES

Because wards are so utterly dependent and vulnerable, they are magnets for regular abuse and exploitation. Experts have suggested that families remain as vigilant as possible to impede or even prevent abuse of their loved ones. They suggest that victimized families listen closely to complaints from wards. Sudden changes in mood, lack of hygiene, swelling, and new wounds or bruising are all red flags that may indicate abuse and should be photographed and documented if possible.

Recording important conversations with administration and staff may uncover a manipulation of facts and reveal a pattern of abuse and exploitation. This type of evidence is valuable when reporting abuse to authorities or documenting it for a judge in an effort to remove abusive guardians.

case. Sadly, stories abound about probate lawyers who happily take large retainers but produce very little in the way of effective legal work.

This point is illustrated by a conversation I recently had with one of the most powerful attorneys in my state, one sympathetic to the issue of guardianship abuse reform, who was asked by another equally important attorney for a referral for representation of a friend who was involved in a pending "friendly guardianship" hearing. Before he made his recommendation, he urgently called me to vet the attorney he planned to propose to see if she was one of the abusive lawyers I had encountered or whether he would be safe in recommending her.

Even when lawyers are earnest and do good work for their clients, it is only very rarely that their pleadings result in hoped-for outcomes for families and wards. Litigation takes a very long time. Judges' dockets are overloaded with guardianships cases, which always seem to bounce back into endless hearings, making them unpopular with the very judges that created them in the first place.

Of course, the longer litigation matters continue, the more likely it is that lawyers will demand further retainers, all the while producing progressively less impactful work. The disappointment that comes with each successive legal failure in probate court is a bitter and very expensive pill to swallow, but many families spend their last dollars on a succession of lawyers in the hope that things might change. A 2015 AAAPG survey revealed that, in some cases, families hire as many as ten attorneys or more in a desperate attempt to save their loved ones, only to be defeated, impoverished, and humiliated by half-hearted, ineffective counsel in a system in favor of the creation and continuation of guardianships.

The impact of this level of constant stress and anxiety is profound. Karin Huffer, MS, has written extensively on what she refers to as "legal abuse syndrome" in her book, *Overcoming the Devastation of Legal Abuse Syndrome.* Huffer shows evidence that protracted litigation is extremely hazardous to health. She offers numerous case studies demonstrating the invisible cumulative stressors from dealing with the justice system.

The victimization generated and perpetuated by the court system is well-documented and validates so many victims of guardianship abuse who have experienced devastation of their belief systems as a result of court involvement. Legal abuse syndrome is real—a variant of PTSD, or post-traumatic stress disorder—and is a diagnosis actually covered by most insurance. It also qualifies under the Americans with Disabilities Act for accommodations when needed. Persistent legal abuse produces profound and hard-to-treat emotional and psychiatric issues, but it also negatively affects blood pressure, diabetes, heart function, and, of course, depression.

The ripple effects of legal abuse not only hurt families for generations but also are costly to society. The resources, energy, time, and effort required to fight guardianship are forever lost when they could have resulted in a benefit to society, and at the very least, the continuation of loving relationships within it. The financial, emotional, and psychological damage heaped on family members who must watch the humiliation, degradation, and ultimate destruction of a loved one leaves scars that never heal. Over 90 percent of the respondents to our 2015 survey indicated that guardianship had destroyed their families.

CONCLUSION

The shockwaves that emanate from an abusive guardianship damage not only the ward involved but also those close to her. An abusive guardianship poses legal, financial, emotional, and psychological challenges that can destroy the strongest of individuals and the best of families. Just the amount of time necessary to deal with the overwhelming amount of legal paperwork is enough to detract from family obligations and activities. Opportunities for relaxation, which is so necessary during times of stress, and valuable time spent with children and grandchildren disappear. Instead of being able to turn to family for support and love, guardianship intentionally and cruelly turns family members against one another, often permanently. Guardianship can lead to life-altering harm that compounds the loss of a loved one.

From the moment a person becomes a ward until after her body is disposed of, the guardianship industry is there to make money. And while there are guardians who are not abusive and may actually act in the best interests of their wards, there are more than enough predatory, even sadistic, guardians to justify the conclusion that guardianship is a direct threat to innocent individuals in every state of this country. In guardianship, the dream of one's "golden years" can be replaced in an instant by a nightmare that continues even after death.

PART 3

Fighting the System

15

Probate
Traps & Tricks

"The post-mortem squabblings and contests
on mental condition . . . have made a will
the least secure of all human dealings."
—LLOYD V. WAYNE CIRCUIT JUDGE, 23 N.W. 28, 30
(MICH. 1885)

Some of the most infuriating parts of the guardianship process are the traps and tricks that court insiders play on unsuspecting litigants and unprepared lawyers. Each of these tactics can make a significant difference in the outcome of a guardianship. These traps are intentionally sprung at inopportune moments, such as when a litigant is known to be going on vacation, before a holiday, on an anniversary or birthday, or at any time that might not be conducive to an effective response. The following examples of probate traps and tricks are typical in guardianship court.

LEGAL TRAPS

There are a number of legal traps that families of wards are at high risk of falling into during guardianship proceedings. For example, *depositions* are supposed to be fact-finding exercises that occur during the "discovery phase" of a case. They are extremely expensive, as multiple lawyers bill their hourly fees while they take turns asking any questions (most of which are barely relevant to the case but great for running up billable hours) they can possibly think of. Their true purpose is to catch a witness in any possible lie and use it against him. Depositions grind down litigants and interested parties, impoverish them, and typically add very little to the issue of who should become guardians, who should be labeled as incapacitated, or whether one side or another has committed wrongdoing of any kind.

Ex parte is a legal term that refers to instances in which a judge makes a decision without all parties involved in the case being present. All too frequently, unannounced and sometimes patently illegal (for failure to notify opposing counsel) private office discussions with a judge lead to important decisions that offer no opportunity for the other party to oppose them or even know about them until after the fact.

When it comes to legal fees, it seems almost any amount can be justified. If fees are challenged, it is common for guardians and their attorneys to rationalize their exorbitant costs by bringing in expert after expert, all paid for by the estate, of course, to testify that these charges are proper and correct and should be paid in full. Often, these experts work in the same courtroom and are well known to the insider community.

Judges are moved from court to court for a variety of reasons. If a judge is moved mid-case, a new judge, who knows nothing about the months of previous litigation, will have to be filled in on the details while he studies his newly assigned trial. His opinions, impressions, and tendencies may be completely different than those of the prior judge, thus lending another layer of unpredictability to probate court proceedings.

Perjury refers to lying in court while under oath. If a lawyer lies in court, it is called a mistake, for which there is no penalty. If a lawyer is caught in a lie, all he has to do is apologize to the judge and the matter is closed, as unlike you or I, lawyers are not under oath in hearings. Moreover, family members who have been maligned and had their characters assassinated never get a chance to repudiate the allegations made against them. Such smears, of course, can greatly affect the outcome of a case.

Federal Rule of Civil Procedure 11 provides that a district court may sanction attorneys or parties who submit pleadings for improper purposes, or which contain frivolous arguments or arguments that have no evidentiary support. Both laypeople and attorneys may be fined, sanctioned, or ordered to pay opposing attorney fees for allegedly violating rules against "abuse of process" or "malicious prosecution," penalties that used to be for lawyers only. Threats of sanctions are common among warring attorneys in guardianship cases.

When you cannot afford an attorney and are forced to represent yourself in hearings (known as *pro se*), you are likely to be treated especially badly by a judge. You may also be found to be a "vexatious litigant"—a judge tactic designed to take away court access from someone he considers a nuisance to a case.

Judges may sanction citizens in court for behavior that court insiders might display without punishment. When supposedly neutral judges show blatant disrespect or contempt for court outsiders in probate court, there is a serious problem with the system.

INCAPACITY CONUNDRUMS

Incapacity is a fluid and poorly defined concept. What is considered incapacity one day may be considered normal activity the next. By manipulating this variable, it can become very easy for a judge to declare a capacitated person incapacitated. For example, an overmedicated AIP may appear incapacitated just prior to his hearing but return to capacity once the effects of the drugs have worn off.

Although examiners have plenty of time to schedule examinations in professional settings and at reasonable times, often these determinations take place at the last minute in public places such as coffee shops or shopping malls. Outside of safe, familiar home settings, wards are more likely to be frightened and perform poorly on these examinations, ultimately resulting in determinations of incapacity.

As mentioned in Chapter 5, a court may invoke emergency temporary guardianship over someone who has suddenly been deemed incapacitated due to illness, injury, or other conditions. Although this power is intended to prevent any harm from being done to an allegedly incapacitated person, this decision is also a surprise tactic, catching family members off guard and preventing or denying them the time necessary to take measures to hire competent representation and prepare essential evidence.

GUARDIANSHIP COMPLICATIONS

Guardianships are intended, by default, to be non-adversarial—meaning both sides should be working cooperatively to achieve an outcome that is best for everyone involved. Unless a case is declared adversarial at the outset, it is possible for a probate attorney to attempt to nullify any attempt to terminate or contest a guardianship by claiming that the guardianship was never affirmed to be adversarial in the first place.

An initial inventory of assets is required in every guardianship case, but creation of this inventory is done in secret and without supervision, meaning that items can conveniently be left off the initial list or subsequent inventories and simply disappear. There is no recourse to question an inventory once it has been approved by a court. Similarly, when it comes time to distribute inventory at the end of a guardianship, typically after the death of a ward, items may suddenly be lost or misplaced and never recovered after years of storage.

A clever way to clear the way for rapid guardianship is to question the authenticity of advance directives. There is no end to the number of ways to cast doubt on documents that were created years earlier, and such doubt allows judges latitude to nullify them. One of the ways advance directives may be thrown out is for a judge to claim that they were written either under undue influence or during a time when the ward in question was already incapacitated but not showing it yet. This is an assertion that cannot be easily disproven.

SILENCING THE FAMILY

After years of litigation, the family members of a ward are generally desperate to settle any outstanding issues, regain their sanity, and restart their lives. Before court insiders agree to settle, however, they will typically insist on non-disparagement and non-disclosure agreements, which prevent family members from complaining about or even mentioning their ordeal under threat of further litigation. This effectively silences family members for good unless they are willing to risk another set of lawsuits.

One very effective way to hush a family member in litigation is to argue that he is not an *interested party*, meaning he has no say in the proceedings. This is a blatant double standard, of course, as bringing an incapacity determination request does not require an individual to be an interested party.

The family member that has been fulfilling the obligation of taking care of a loved one is the most likely target of accusations of *undue influence*. Every horrible thing possible will be said about him in order to prove that he is unworthy of acting as a guardian and to remove him as a barrier to private guardianship. The family member who has given the most to the loved one is also the one who will get the least of the estate inheritance but the most legal abuse.

If family members complain too vociferously and become too much of a nuisance to probate insiders, the quickest and most vicious way to silence them is to prevent them from even seeing their loved one, which is accomplished by claims that their presence upsets the ward or is a threat to his safety. This outrageous leverage may be illegal in many states, but it is one of the most commonly used weapons in probate.

CONCLUSION

These are just a few of the tricks of the trade well known to probate insiders. Using these methods, court insiders may tilt the playing field drastically in their favor when confronted by opposition that is not even in their league. Combine these tricks with the long-standing relationships and repayment of favors that exist in probate court and guardianship proceedings suddenly seem like a stacked deck, a rigged game in which the only winners are court insiders.

16

Preventing & Fighting Guardianship

"Injustice anywhere is a threat to justice everywhere."
—Martin Luther King, Jr.

When a court acts in ways that are contrary to what we have been told to believe about American justice, we are then forced to suspend our trust in the system and prepare to exercise all our options to obtain justice and preserve lives and assets. But preventing or contesting a guardianship can be an unbelievably difficult task, and the freedoms and rights we all take for granted are nearly impossible to retrieve once stripped away by guardianship.

Fighting an abusive guardianship takes an incredible amount of effort, perseverance, and courage, as well as the ability to deal with repeated failure and speak truth to power fearlessly. It requires exceptional record-keeping and organizational skills, extraordinary emotional resilience, above-average communication skills, online access, and, most importantly, support from others. It also takes lots of time and money.

Asking state government for relief is a maddening exercise. Law enforcement will adamantly refuse to take reports of guardianship abuse, claiming, contrary to most statutes, that the issue is civil and that a lawyer must be retained to deal with the matter in court. Politicians of all stripes and even their employees may be very sympathetic to these types of complaints, but legislators are in office to pass laws, and passing laws takes a great deal of money and time, of which advocate litigants in probate court have limited amounts.

Advocates quickly discover that the bar and judicial complaint systems are incapable of seeing their points of view or the gravity of their complaints. These self-anointed complaint departments are not inclined to act against the best interests of their memberships unless the actions of the judges or attorneys in question are so publicly egregious that they are compelled to do something to retain the public trust.

Streams of complaints have flowed to the United States Senate Select Subcommittee on Aging in regard to guardianship over the last forty years. There had been no federal action taken (possibly because of the probate exception) on any aspect of elder abuse until the passage of Senate Bill 178 by Senators Grassley and Klobuchar, which was recently signed into law by President Trump. One can only hope that it is the first proper step towards better record-keeping and an understanding of the abuse that occurs on a regular basis in guardianship probate cases across the country.

To be blunt, there have been no effective official complaint departments for a very long time. Florida's Office of Public and Professional Guardians (OPPG) was created after advocates from AAAPG lobbied for its creation. It is purely an administrative channel for complaints from the public and is empowered to impose mild sanctions (not criminal) on guardians who violate guidelines.

PREVENTING A GUARDIANSHIP

Since fighting a guardianship process that has already begun is such a hard task, the absolute best way to deal with the dangers of guardianship is to prevent one before it starts. Basing these suggestions on their real-life experiences, members of AAAPG have shared a number of tactics with which to take precautions against guardianship and advocate for a loved one. What follows is not legal advice but practical considerations for those who find themselves in a pre-probate predicament. Although it may seem like a lot of work, even overkill, to read through all this advice in connection with something that is still only a threat, the reality is bad enough to warrant the preparation, no matter the likelihood of it coming to fruition.

Upon discovering any hint of the threat of guardianship of a loved one, do the following as soon as possible:

1. Proactively gather all parties and resolve all family disputes before they escalate into a tragic guardianship situation. No matter what you give up in doing so, it will be far cheaper than any guardianship. And it may save your loved one's life. Convince everyone that failure to reach an agreed-upon accommodation could mean that everyone will lose their inheritances and their loved one, too. Sadly, this is rarely possible in families with severe dysfunction. Unless you have absolutely no other choice, however, never ask a lawyer to solve family disputes. Never believe that your interests and concerns are more important to a lawyer than her own interests. Do not believe that facts and truth always succeed in court. If there is evidence of abuse of any kind from a family member, report it to the police, not to Adult Protective Services or a lawyer.

2. Execute and file your loved one's "next level" advance directives, including a video expressing the wishes of the potential ward as well as documentation of her capacity. If assistance is needed, it is best to receive it from a non-family member so as to avoid allegations of undue influence from family. Be sure these directives:

   • make it clear that the potential ward expressly forbids the appointment of a professional guardian under any circumstances.

- demand that the court of jurisdiction for any potential guardianship matter be located in the ward's district at the time of notification of incapacity determination. (This is an escape clause for those living in guardianship "hotspots," allowing them time to move to a different jurisdiction and possibly avoid guardianship.)

- assert that mediation is to be considered as a substitute for any formal proceedings in court.

- name at least six individuals who would be acceptable if the absolute need for guardianship should arise. They need not be family members.

- provide up-to-date notarized copies of all of your loved one's end-of-life wishes, as well as her video, to every relevant member of your family and all medical providers and hospitals, as well as an attorney, so there is no likelihood that they will be unavailable when needed.

- include digital copies of information and documents in PDF format to prevent unwanted tampering or editing.

Do your best to make all family members aware that your loved one expects her wishes to be followed without exception.

3. Obtain a valid notarized comprehensive Medical Certificate of Capacity for your loved one from a physician, preferably a specialist in neuroscience, and update it regularly. A link to this document is available at the end of this book. (See page 218.) Include this completed certificate in your packet of advance directives.

4. Advise your loved one to limit her visits to financial personnel, such as banks, brokerages, or credit unions, to avoid overeager employees reporting transactions to agencies like Adult Protective Services in a misguided effort to protect their customers. Financial institutions now have a duty to report suspicious transactions, particularly those of elderly people, who are often

victims of scams and exploitation. (A transaction such as a withdrawal of a large amount of cash would be a red flag.) When visits are unavoidable, seniors should deal only with known employees of a financial institution and be accompanied by a trusted family member, who can supervise and validate legitimate financial transactions.

5. Whenever possible, place your loved one's assets in joint tenancy accounts. It is much harder for the court to seize these accounts than any others.

6. If your loved one has a spouse or family member living with her who is listed as an heir to her mortgaged property, be sure to have the name of this spouse or family member listed as a co-mortgagor on the mortgage document. Doing so will allow this person to continue to occupy the property without interruption and prevent eviction by a guardian or bank.

7. Get your loved one out of town. Because preparations for guardianship can begin in secret long before anyone is aware of them, and because guardianships are often sprung on naïve, unsuspecting families and seniors when they least expect them, should anyone even offhandedly mention the possibility of guardianship in any setting, *recognize this as an emergency.* Remove your loved one to another state, where she will establish new residency to escape jurisdiction. Do not delay.

There are certain steps that an elderly person moving to a new state due to threat of guardianship should take to establish residency quickly and effectively. This person should:

• locate a place to live in the state. Even a motel will do temporarily. Ideally, she should move in with a trusted family member or friend. If necessary, she should move into an undisclosed assisted living facility—not a nursing home, which will require her to give all his personal information, making it very easy to find her.

- obtain a new government ID or driver's license and register to vote in her new location. She will likely need two other forms of ID to do so (e.g., utility bills, credit card statements, etc.).

- redirect delivery of her social security or any other benefits to her new location.

- be prepared to spend at least 184 days in her chosen state to qualify for residency.

- begin and maintain social and business relations in the new state.

- open at least one account in the new state at a bank different from and not related to her current one.

- establish a new mailing address with the United States Postal Service by going to the nearest post office and filing a change of address form.

- have her important documents and all mail redirected to her new address (insurance, memberships, licenses, etc.)

- file tax returns and pay taxes in the state in which she is establishing residency.

- perform a comprehensive inventory of all assets that includes as much information as possible about locations, markets, current and replacement values, acquisition costs, and dates. If a guardianship is instituted at some point, this baseline inventory will serve as a safeguard against the creation of a fraudulent inventory by a guardian. Copies of most recent bank statements should be procured. Photographs of assets should be included along with any formal appraisals that exist. This inventory should be stored in her advance directives packet along with enough cash to last at least two weeks, a supply of all medications, and her passport and driver's license.

- obtain an up-to-date comprehensive medical record from her healthcare provider, including all medications taken and, in particular, the results of any studies done for neurological purposes, including CAT scans and MRIs. This private record should reside only in her advance directive packet. All relevant telephone numbers of caregivers, pharmacies, and durable medical equipment suppliers should be listed. This entire packet should be safely stored, preferably in an organized, indexed, and clearly marked binder, readily accessible in an urgent situation.

• place all credit cards on hold to prevent her being tracked and any unmonitored use of her assets. Once residency has been established, these cards can be reactivated.

• not inform anyone of her destination until new residency is established. If existing advance directives state that jurisdiction rests in the location of her current residence, the court may try to force her to return. Once residency has been established in a new state that is not a guardianship hotspot, she may consider returning to her prior residence.

Establishing residency may be done in the same general manner in all fifty states. Anyone seeking to establish residency in a new state should go online to see its specific obligations for acquiring resident status, such as the length of time one must reside in the state to qualify as a legal resident. If you are able to do this research in advance of moving yourself or your loved one, do so.

FIGHTING AN EXISTING GUARDIANSHIP

Once the guardianship process has begun with the court issuance of letters of guardianship (also called letters of office or guardianship commission), time is your enemy. Each day that passes reduces the odds of reversing course. Every move court insiders make is designed to place obstacles in front of any challenge to guardianship. And after a ward's assets have been confiscated, she will have no resources left to assist her family in the acquisition of adequate legal representation to fight this battle.

Finding ways to fight guardianship in order to save a loved one and her assets is anything but easy or straightforward. But it is very important. The grantors of inheritances fully expect their assets to be distributed to their descendants, not to lawyers and guardians.

Resisting Guardianship Players

Since the system is so complex and intricate, it makes some sense to attack each foundational component of it separately. Causing the failure of any one aspect of the guardianship system might just destroy it as a whole. The following suggestions are not legal advice but instead are practical methodologies that have had some degree of success in certain guardianship fights in the past. These actions may be undertaken by an individual but are best performed with the support of a group of like-minded people and an honest, motivated attorney. Any one or more of the following approaches, when applied intelligently and persistently, might be enough to convince court insiders to give in and abandon the fight.

The Guardian and Company

You may demand financial and criminal background checks on any individual assigned by a court to play any role in a guardianship. Anyone who refuses or whose records turn up anomalies should be replaced by the court.

You may also demand evidence of a guardian's bonding and certification. Search legal records for evidence of suits against her for misconduct in guardianship. Guardians may also be replaced for failure to report personal bankruptcies or felonies. Any errors or evidence of even the smallest type of wrongdoing are grounds to demand a guardian's dismissal and replacement.

Look for irregularities in the licensure of any individual who comes into direct contact with your loved one under guardianship, particularly medical personnel and home health aides. There are often inconsistencies and inaccuracies in their records. Ask for formal evidence of all caregivers' liability insurance or bonding—usually a tipoff that you are about to sue them. Bring any irregularities immediately to the court in a petition to dismiss the individuals in question and their companies.

The Examining Committee

Keep a close eye on examining committee members. Get copies of all their reports. Make sure that the physician on the three-member panel is actually licensed in your state. The same goes for any social workers or other professionals on the examining committee. Research any lawsuits against them outside of the guardianship sphere that would raise doubts about their reliability or integrity. Demand a hearing to interrogate the examining committee members, whose stories will often be inconsistent and occasionally incoherent. Point out the inconsistencies of time actually spent with the ward versus time billed to the court. Any inconsistencies discovered are grounds for tossing the entire report.

The Attorney

I do not recommend attacking the legitimacy of guardian's attorney. Doing so would cause pointless litigation, which would be profitable to this same attorney. Unless you have concrete evidence of illegal behavior, court immunity will protect the lawyer every time. All it will do for you is cause financial ruin. Objecting to her fees, however, is another matter. Scour fee requests for duplicate charges and excessive billing hours and object to every suspicious entry.

Resisting the Court System

There are a number of ways to fight against the court system responsible for creating abusive guardianships.

- Attack through law enforcement. Be persistent and demand case reports be made by local police on guardian abuses you can document. These are needed for filing any future criminal actions and are a real weapon in slowing down attacks on the family.

- Attack through the media. Media attention is the last thing court insiders want. It can be an effective tool when confronted with abuse that can be exposed by the media.

- Attack the court record. Always hire your own court reporter. You will find that there are often discrepancies between your version of events in hearings and the "official" version, which has been known to be altered at times.

- Attack the financial reports. Never accept opposing counsel's forensic accounting without a challenge. Review the information in great detail and challenge every single inaccuracy to disqualify the entire document. Engage a professional forensic accountant familiar with probate abuse, which can be invaluable in building a case against a fallacious report.

- Attack the judge if she is biased against you. Document evidence that supports the notion that you can never get a fair shake from her and then formally request that she recuse herself from the case. Most state laws require a judge to step down from a case if such a complaint has been deemed valid.

- Attack through the district courts of appeal. Appeal every adverse decision as soon as it is made. At the very least, this will slow down the probate process. There is a fifty-fifty chance your appeal will be taken and perhaps even resolved in your favor.

- Attack through the federal courts. Document your complaints using the Department of Justice complaint form and hope that help will come in the form of Elder Justice Task Force Investigators. This may be one way to circumvent the Eleventh Amendment, which prevents the federal government from intervening in most cases of guardianship in state courts. Cases are being filed around the country testing this approach.

- Attack to negate jurisdiction by moving the ward in question to a different state, as described earlier in this chapter.

Appealing a Decision

Our legal system was founded on the ability to seek justice at multiple levels of the judiciary, from lower courts on up. When a decision seems wrong or inappropriate, a citizen can lodge an appeal.

Fighting an unacceptable lower court decision can be an incredibly complex matter and exposes the appellant to another layer of our convoluted justice system. The intricate issues of court appeals are beyond the scope of this book, but appeals of probate decisions are limited by the fact that appellate courts may decline to hear them. In regard to appealing a particular ruling within a larger case, if an appellate court accepts this appeal, the associated lower court is basically frozen in place until the appeal has been adjudicated. Theoretically, this means the case in question stops. In practice, however, the dozens of aspects unrelated to the appeal of a specific ruling may continue to be litigated and often are.

SOURCES OF LEGAL ASSISTANCE

Most litigants in probate are drained of funds fairly rapidly and forced into situations in which they can no longer afford representation. Law school clinics may be of assistance in these matters, assigning senior law students to these cases under the supervision of law school professors. Pro bono lawyers, who do not charge clients for their services, are often made available by the state bar for those individuals who cannot afford their own attorneys. Usually these are younger attorneys with little experience but certainly more knowledge and insight into the law than the average citizen. Occasionally, it is possible to find an effective attorney who, if she thinks your case is winnable, will share the risk with you and represent you on contingency in return for up to 50 percent of any recovery.

Even if an appellate court finds in an appellant's favor, it may do so only partially. Moreover, the judge of the associated lower court may ignore this ruling altogether, thus forcing the appellant to pay more legal fees to obtain a *writ of mandamus,* which is designed to compel a judicial or governmental officer to perform a duty owed to a petitioner.

Litigants who have tried but failed to obtain redress for their grievances through the normal complaint mechanisms and feel the court system has ignored or violated federal laws may consider filing a complaint with the Department of Justice. While this option seems logical and sensible based on a layman's understanding of the law, appealing to the federal government for relief from state courts is an extremely complex and often disappointing undertaking. There are a number of barriers involved in enlisting the federal government to intervene in guardianship litigation. There is a large body of case law tilted in favor of states retaining jurisdiction and avoiding federal intervention, particularly in guardianship cases.

With the recent passage of federal legislation on elder abuse in guardianship matters, however, there is renewed interest in pursuing federal remedies to guardianship court abuses. This interest focuses mainly on overcoming the Eleventh Amendment to the Constitution, which prevents the federal government from intervening in most cases of guardianship in state courts.

A new strategy may, in fact, allow a litigant to circumvent the Eleventh Amendment. It leverages the fact that the court system that comprises guardianship sometimes receives funding from the federal government in the form of grants and awards. When a court accepts federal funds of any kind it is then forced to abide by what is called the Supremacy Clause of the United States Constitution. Under the Supremacy Clause, state laws or actions that violate federal law are invalid, including civil rights violations. A case could be made that probate court actions that violate federal civil rights laws in a state court system that receives federal funds are actually invalid. For those who can still afford legal representation, this approach might be worth discussing with counsel.

CONCLUSION

Guardianships are much easier to prevent than to fight once instituted. The best guardianship is the one that never happens because
family members realize that it would rob them not only of their
loved one but also their inheritances. The guardianship industry
is well organized, well funded, politically empowered, and judicially protected. Fighting it requires enormous courage, tenacity,
and powerful legal representation.

Court insiders are used to winning and will fight to the last to
protect their turf, their power, and, of course, their money. They
cannot afford even a single defeat for fear that their system of
abuse will be exposed and their gravy train will end. Any insider
careless enough to be caught and convicted, like April Parks or
Patience Bristol in Nevada, is thrown under the proverbial bus as
an outlier and not representative of the industry as a whole. The
entire guardianship apparatus aligns against its opponents and
is not used to being challenged—and certainly not to losing. But
things can change.

17

Alternative Dispute Resolution

"You can't solve problems until you understand the other side."
—Jeffrey Manber, CEO of Nanoracks

For potential guardianship litigants, viable alternatives to probate court procedures or decisions may be preferable to the typical mess of guardianship proceedings. These alternatives are forms of a technique known as *alternative dispute resolution,* which is becoming more and more popular in guardianship battles.

When a guardianship is contested, court proceedings are sometimes used as a weapon by those involved rather than as a means to determine what is best for an allegedly incapacitated person, and there is little incentive for any party to disarm. Other times, a matter is contested as a result of a miscommunication, or a lack of communication, between parties. Whatever the case, such contested proceedings are an abusive waste of a court's time and a needless strain on a family's resources.

Additionally, proceedings can be severely embarrassing, often putting a family's dirty laundry on public display. The battle for control over an allegedly incapacitated person's estate can turn a courtroom into a forum for the airing and avenging of perceived wrongs, no matter how large or small, real or imagined.

Contested guardianship cases are frequently lose-lose scenarios. Although someone eventually emerges as the "winner" by judicial decree, this victory comes at too high a cost. In truth, everyone involved in guardianship litigation ends up as a loser. The process only deepens the wounds that lead to the contest in the first place, after which there is even less of a chance of them healing. At best, the parties share a queasy coexistence out of mutual concern for the incapacitated person, but the family of the litigants is irreparably destroyed.

OUTSIDE THE COURTROOM

Alternative dispute resolution (ADR) refers to any means of settling disputes outside of the courtroom. ADR techniques applicable to guardianship litigation include but are not limited to conciliation, mediation, and arbitration. As burgeoning court dockets, outrageous costs of litigation, and time delays continue to frustrate and enrage litigants, some states have begun experimenting with ADR court diversion programs. Some of these programs are voluntary; others are mandatory.

While the two most common forms of ADR are mediation and arbitration, some type of informal negotiation is almost always attempted first to resolve a dispute. Negotiation allows the concerned parties to meet in order to settle a disagreement. The main advantage of this form of dispute settlement is that it permits the involved parties to control the process and solution themselves. Once guardianship litigation has begun in earnest, typically multiple attempts at informal negotiation among the parties have taken place and failed.

Conciliation

Conciliation is an informal, out-of-court technique in which parties seek to reach an amicable dispute settlement with the assistance of a conciliator, who acts as a neutral third party. Conciliation is a voluntary, confidential process that allows the parties involved to attempt to resolve their dispute in a friendly manner. It is a flexible process, allowing the parties to define the time, structure, and content of the proceedings in ways most convenient for them. The conciliator takes into account the parties' legal positions, as well as their personal and financial interests. Conciliation is rarely seen in guardianship cases due to its structural limitations and the fact that the stakes are so high for the opposing sides.

Mediation

Mediation is a slightly more formal alternative to litigation. Court-appointed mediators are individuals trained in negotiations that bring opposing parties together and attempt to reach a settlement or agreement between parties. In guardianship matters, mediators are typically court insiders, usually retired probate judges. The mediation process is highly unpredictable, and there is no guarantee that a retired judge will have more interest in solving a guardianship issue than one who is still on the bench. The process is, however, quite profitable for retired judges, who can bill even more than lawyers.

Many attorneys, and most laypeople, confuse mediation with other forms of alternative dispute resolution. Mediation is a voluntary and confidential discussion between parties with the aim of resolving the conflict between them. The mediator's role is to facilitate this discussion. He has no power to decide on issues, unlike a judge, arbitrator, or early neutral evaluator. Since mediation is confidential, parties agree that the mediator cannot be subpoenaed to testify on anyone's behalf. They also agree not to divulge or voluntarily testify about anything said during the course of the mediation. The mediator collects and destroys all notes taken during mediation, including his own notes. Moreover, most courts prohibit statements made during settlement negotiations from being introduced into evidence. Therefore, no party prejudices its position by engaging in mediation.

Ideally, a mediation session takes place in a neutral setting. A typical mediation session begins with a brief opening statement by the mediator, followed by the commencement of dialogue between the parties. During this session, the mediator may meet privately with each party in what is known as a *caucus*. The contents of a caucus are confidential between the mediator and particular party unless and until this party authorizes the mediator to divulge what was said. Of course, the other parties are entitled to equal time in caucus with the mediator.

A mediation session can last anywhere from one to several hours. The session terminates when the parties reach an agreement, or when either party wishes to terminate. Bear in mind, since mediation is voluntary, there is little point in trying if the parties do not, in good faith, desire to resolve their differences, as is so often the case in contested guardianships.

An agreement may be oral or written. A written agreement is considered a binding stipulation or contract and can be the basis of judicial enforcement of its terms. That the parties do not reach an oral or written agreement does not mean that the mediation session was a failure. The parties may well leave the session with a new understanding of the other participants' perceptions, points of view, needs, goals, and desires. This alone may cause a party to alter his position or narrow the issues remaining to be litigated, facilitating resolution of the matter.

Mediation can be especially valuable in cases of contested guardianship. If a potential ward's family feels that an appointed guardian may not act in his best interests, mediation can help resolve this concern before it comes to litigation. Unfortunately, long-standing family feuds and dysfunction often derail even the best attempts at mediation. For an interested party to have a sudden change of heart based on a third party's intervention is unlikely. Mediation creates additional expenses to the already outrageous costs associated with probate litigation. Furthermore, even if an agreement is reached, a probate judge may nullify it at any time. The results of successful mediation may be approved only by his ruling.

READ CAREFULLY

Always be sure to read a settlement very carefully. Final settlements that are designed to conclude legal matters may be booby-trapped in court documents and need to be appealed. In too many cases, lawyers fail to inform their clients about certain clauses they have incorporated into their settlement agreements, such as agreeing not to sue any of the lawyers or guardians involved. There may also be clauses that prevent defamation or even public mention of the litigants involved.

Arbitration

Arbitration is a simplified, somewhat stripped-down version of a trial. It involves limited discovery and simplified rules of evidence. The big difference is that it does not necessarily involve judges. Arbitration is headed and decided by an arbitral panel. To comprise a panel, either both sides agree on one arbitrator, or each side selects one arbitrator and these two individuals elect a third.

Arbitration hearings usually last between a few days and one week, and the panel only meets for a few hours per day. The panel then deliberates and issues a written decision, or arbitral award. Settlements and arbitration are binding, and if the outcome of arbitration is unsatisfactory to one or the other party, there are very few options to overturn it. Arbitration is rarely employed in guardianship cases unless it has been incorporated into advance directives.

Probate court has become a place so unpredictable that leading attorneys and estate planning professionals, as well as their clients, want to avoid it at all costs. Arbitration has become a popular way to resolve disputes that often arise in contested guardianship cases because it is designed to reduce litigation.

Juan C. Antúnez, Esq., a noted Miami Probate Specialist, writes:

> If you ask the average estate-planning professional why he or she thinks it is a good idea to "avoid probate," the costs, delays, and lack of privacy inherent to our state operated system of probate

administration will likely top the list. As real as those concerns may be in uncontested probate proceedings, they take on epic proportions if litigation breaks out . . . estate litigation poses a much greater risk to family wealth than the focus of much estate planning today, which is taxes. Today, 99.8 percent of estates owe *no estate tax at all.* By contrast, the potential wealth-destroying risk posed by estate litigation is exponentially greater and widespread. According to a study cited by the WSJ in a piece entitled *When Heirs Collide*, it is a risk that actually impacts close to 70 percent of all families.

By shifting to arbitration and privatizing the dispute-resolution process whenever possible, concerned parties can avoid the pitfalls inherent to an overworked and underfunded public court system. For example, in Miami-Dade County, each probate judge takes on, on average, 3,069 new cases a year. In Broward County, the figure is even higher, at 3,899 cases per judge. Palm Beach County scores the lowest, at 1,950 cases per judge.

The caseload figures often seen in larger counties may be appropriate for uncontested proceedings, but when it comes to the subset of estates that *are* litigated, these same statistics (confirmed by personal experience) make it glaringly clear that we are not doing our jobs as estate planners if we do not anticipate and plan accordingly for the structural limitations of our public court system.

Arbitration is surely imperfect, but at least you get some say in who is going to decide your case and what his minimum qualifications need to be. And in the arbitration process, which is privately funded, you also have a fighting chance of getting your arbitrator to actually read your briefs and invest the time and mental focus needed to evaluate the complex tax law, state law, and family dynamics underlying the case. Such is a luxury that is all but impossible in a state court system that forces judges to juggle thousands of cases at a time with little or no support.

If arbitration can be used to prevent guardianship proceedings, it may be worth adding it to advance directives. Unfortunately, arbitration may also create a trap if it turns out to be one-sided, as it sometimes does, and results in an enforceable settlement that is unsatisfactory.

CONCLUSION

It is becoming increasingly clear that probate equity court proceedings are flawed and beset with irreconcilable conflicts of interest, which are generally exposed in high-value cases. The stakes in such litigation are extremely high, with huge amounts of money administered in probate proceedings. While probate may function nominally under certain circumstances, when overworked judges in an underfunded system deal with extended estate litigation, the likelihood of abuse and exploitation rises dramatically. Families are frequently disenfranchised and subject to abuse and the loss of huge amounts of their assets.

While some guardianship disputes may be resolved by the use of different forms of alternative dispute resolution, today thousands upon thousands of new guardianships are routinely created. In certain guardianship cases, alternative resolution dispute methods may be effective in settling disagreements privately, promptly, and economically. Sadly, in most problematic cases, none of these techniques are ever used.

Conclusion

*"We cannot expect people to have respect for law
and order until we teach respect to those we
have entrusted to enforce those laws."*
—HUNTER S. THOMPSON, WRITER

We are a country of laws. Laws are the glue that holds our democratic republic together. Laws create a framework for our everyday actions, dictate the protections that government affords us, and define the responsibilities that earn us the right to these protections.

In our system of government, state statutes are always subject to federal law, with the exception of probate rulings in inheritances and guardianships. This unique situation puts a wall in front of the possibility of appealing a probate decision to federal court or the Department of Justice. It also makes the lowest state equity-type courts and, in particular, guardianship courts, the places in which the vast majority of guardianship decisions, post-death property transfers, trust or estate matters, and a vast array of other critically important issues are finalized. It makes judges in these courts incredibly powerful.

History repeatedly teaches us that absolute power corrupts absolutely. History also shows us that those in power often develop an addiction to it, will do almost anything to retain it, and will take any steps they deem necessary against those who dare challenge their authority. In many cases, this addiction and hubris grow stronger over time, particularly in those who consistently abuse their power without ever facing the consequences of their actions.

In theory, judicial power is clearly defined in foundational documents that function as safeguards against greed and self-interest, such as our Constitution, Bill of Rights, and our statutes. But when judges are unaware of or uninterested in the rule of law; display bias in spite of facts, laws, or evidence; allow exploitation by their friends who, in turn, keep them in power; and constantly hide their decisions from scrutiny; they expose the need for transparency and dissent to maintain the legitimacy of our courts.

This problem, however, is not only the fault of judges. The rules by which they act are rigged. Probate law has been handed over to unelected, self-interested administrative officials—probate industry attorneys and their associates, banks, and realtors—who are empowered to enact self-serving rules and codes. Arguably, some of these rules are inconsistent with our constitutional protections.

Victims and litigants in all probate cases and settlements are coerced into signing non-disclosure and non-disparaging contracts, which silence them. This is the industry's secret weapon, allowing lawyers to perpetrate fraud with impunity, absent any meaningful supervision, and with the ability to divert assets. When these tactics nullify or override statutes, common law, religion, or moral values, we must speak out.

The systemic dysfunction within some courts, which AAAPG has documented, is glaring. It is not enough simply to call it exploitation or abuse. It is an affront to our American justice system for individuals to be tormented and their families hounded by what is supposed to be a helpful arrangement for the most vulnerable members of our society. Something has to be done, and it must happen now, before courts are flooded with new cases due to the increasing population of elderly people, also known as the "silver tsunami," in the United States.

CHANGING OUR THINKING AND APPROACH

When a judge violates state statutes, we must call this violation what it is: a crime. It is a *crime* for a judge to violate these statutes or claim to be ignorant of them while presiding over and ruling on cases—especially non-jury cases.

It is a *crime* for a judge to turn a blind eye and allow her appointees—especially the lawyers—to blatantly lie, commit fraud, or steal assets that belong to wards. Judges have statutory authority and a mandate to oversee their appointees but consistently fail to supervise the actions of these individuals.

It is a *crime* for a judge to misuse sequestration to hide her or her appointees' ongoing questionable activities, which if discovered would mean their removal from employment. The veil of secrecy that is sequestration has been an almost insurmountable obstacle preventing the audit of judges and their appointees. The lifting of this veil might just reveal the extent to which both parties' finances are intermingled.

It is a *crime* for a judge to allow her appointees—especially the lawyers—to separate wards from their families, loved ones, or beloved pets, isolating and imprisoning them in a loveless environment in which no one could possibly thrive. This failure to provide incapacitated people of any age with basic love, care, and tenderness and allow them to enjoy their lives with dignity is one of the worst crimes that can be committed. Life is precious and should never be treated as dispensable or with such disdain.

It is a *crime* for a judge to allow court insiders to act corruptly. Judges have statutory authority and a mandate to handle cases fairly and impartially but instead consistently refer case matters only to insiders and ignore their exploitation of the parties involved.

Insider judges, lawyers, guardians, and other professionals must be held to the highest standard of propriety and accountability. There is not one set of laws and punishments for insiders and another for everybody else. Unless we all obey the same laws, these laws mean very little. It is the joint responsibility of the Supreme Court, the Department of Justice, and citizens to demand accountability from judges and their court insiders.

We can no longer ignore the horrors of abusive guardianship. The need to recognize these abuses is real and urgent. Dementia rates among baby boomers are projected to rise. An increasing number of vulnerable seniors with significant assets will pose serious challenges to families for whom the responsibility of elder care will be overwhelming.

WHAT TO DO NEXT

Unfortunately, guardianship has gone from a last resort to the only resort. Court-ordered examinations almost never suggest ways of avoiding substituted decision-making. Rather than offer solutions that could help a person maintain her rights, these court-ordered examinations seem to exist primarily to give courts an excuse to exercise their power to create guardianships.

Every potential guardianship case should be prevented whenever possible. This system, which is so prone to corruption, must ultimately be abolished and totally replaced by a more humane approach that is in step with twenty-first-century America. This should be the real challenge to lawmakers, not tinkering with a system that has so easily perverted the law for over forty years.

So, how should we overhaul the system in the short term? And with what should we replace it? First and foremost, the financial incentive to abuse wards would be substantially dampened by enacting stringent caps on legal fees. It is money, not goodwill, which drives the guardianship industry, and eliminating its overabundance in the system would be a transformative action.

The examination system must also be overhauled. There is no excuse for laypeople being able to declare a person incapacitated in the twenty-first century when techniques and experts in the field are readily available. Further, professional assessments of AIPs that contradict those of court examiners must be allowed into evidence and seriously considered by the court. In addition, the concealment of proceedings through sequestration must end. It is absurd to "protect the privacy" of wards when you are about to take away their rights, assets, and life.

Finally, as envisioned by the Elder Justice Task Force, there must be a receptive and functional criminal complaint department with teeth, which can handle matters of abuse and exploitation—which, after all, are crimes. The terrifying reports of wards being starved to death, overmedicated and turned into zombies, impoverished, isolated from family and friends, or abused in facilities show how drastically the current system of judicial oversight has failed us.

The ultimate goal, of course, is to replace guardianship with something far better. Despite the emergence of alternative dispute resolution techniques, supported decision-making, and the efforts of many anti-guardianship advocacy groups, the thorny issue of how we view and assist seniors who have cognitive problems remains a major challenge—one that is rapidly becoming a full-blown crisis.

We must do better, and we must do so now. We must stop considering the removal of an individual's rights as the cost of assistance. We must turn to court-appointed assistance only as a last resort. We must encourage and empower family to resolve conflicts without court intervention. We must never allow advance directives to be nullified. We must hold court insiders criminally liable for their improper acts.

With these foundational concepts in place, a more humane and firm system may evolve and replace the fatally flawed system we have today. America's abusive guardianship system need no longer be an intergenerational problem. I hope this book has opened your eyes to the threat of our guardianship system run amok, the overt criminality within it, and the real need to repeal and replace it. I also hope you will become an advocate for change, if for no other reason than to protect yourself and your loved ones.

Glossary

ad litem. Appointed to act in a lawsuit on behalf of someone who is incapable of representing himself.

advance directives. Also known as advance healthcare directives, this term refers to a collection of approved documents through which a person specifies the actions that should be taken for his benefit or health if he becomes no longer able to make decisions for himself because of illness or incapacity. (These directives typically include documents such as powers of attorney, healthcare proxies, and living wills.)

allegedly incapacitated person (AIP). Person for whom a pre-guardianship incapacity evaluation has been requested or ordered by a court.

alternative dispute resolution (ADR). The settling of disputes using techniques that take place outside the courtroom, which include conciliation, mediation, and arbitration.

appellate court. Court responsible for reviewing appeals of legal cases that have already been tried in court.

beneficiary. Person who is eligible to receive distributions from a trust, will, or insurance policy.

caucus. Private meeting between a mediator and one of the parties involved in mediation.

conservator. Also known as a guardian, this term refers to an individual appointed by the court to protect the health, assets, and welfare of a ward.

court insider. Person who benefits directly or indirectly from court proceedings and who works to keep the system in place.

court of equity. Court that operates on principles of equity, which allow judges to resolve disagreements based on general principles of fairness at their own discretion.

court of law. Court that operates on principles of law. In law cases, the court makes decisions based on a set of established rules.

deposition. Formal, usually written, statement to be used as evidence.

disposition of assets. Act of getting rid of assets or securities through a direct sale or some other method of transfer.

docket. Calendar or list of cases pending.

due process. Right to adequate notice and hearing through the normal judicial system.

emergency temporary guardianship. Guardianship ordered by a judge to provide a ward with immediate protection for a brief period of time.

ex parte. With respect to or in the interests of one side only.

family guardianship. Guardianship in which a family member is appointed guardian, sometimes placed under the supervision of another court-appointed guardian.

frozen asset. Asset that is owned but cannot be sold or used in any way due to a debt that needs to be paid. This asset remains frozen until such debt has been paid.

grantor. Individual who conveys or transfers ownership of property.

healthcare proxy. Document with which a patient appoints an agent to make healthcare decisions on his behalf.

incapacity. Lack of physical or intellectual power, or of natural or legal qualifications.

inventory report. Summary of an estate's assets.

involuntary commitment. Legal process through which an individual who has been deemed by a qualified agent to have symptoms of mental disorder is court-ordered for observation in a psychiatric hospital.

intestate. Not having made a will before one dies.

legal competence. Mental ability to participate in legal proceedings or transactions, and to take responsibility for one's decisions and actions.

letters of guardianship. Documents issued by a judge that legally authorize an individual or company to make decisions on another person's behalf.

limited guardianship. Legal relationship in which an appointed guardian has control only over certain aspects of a person's life.

litigate. Take a claim or dispute to a court of law.

litigant. Person involved in a lawsuit.

living trust. Estate-planning tool used to pass on one's assets and affairs to a particular person in the event of a determination of incapacity while avoiding probate.

notice of hearing. Prepared legal document that invokes all parties to hear a motion and may be emitted by any party.

plenary guardianship. Guardianship in which a person is granted the right to handle all legal decisions on behalf of a ward.

power of attorney. Written authorization to act on another person's behalf in private affairs, business, or some other legal matter.

pro se. Representing oneself in court.

probate court. Court with power over the administration of estates and wills of deceased individuals.

professional guardianship. Guardianship in which a court-approved private guardian, who does this work for a living, is assigned to a ward.

public guardianship. Guardianship in which a guardian is provided to ward through a government assistance program.

sequestration. Keeping court records hidden from the public.

statute. Written law passed by a legislative body.

statutory. Required, permitted, or enacted by statute.

stay away order. Court order stating that a person may not come near or contact another.

substituted decision-making. Approach to guardianship that does not allow a person to make any decisions for himself.

supported decision-making. Approach to guardianship that allows a person to make decisions for himself with assistance from a trusted network of supporters.

surety bonds. Legally binding contract that ensures obligations will be met between three parties: the principal, or whoever needs the bond; the obligee, the one requiring the bond; and the surety, the insurance company guaranteeing the principal can fulfill the obligations.

temporary guardianship. Guardianship that exists for a limited period of time and a specific purpose.

testamentary trust. Trust that arises upon the death of a testator and is specified in his will.

testator. Person who has made a will or given a legacy.

undue influence. Equitable doctrine that involves one person taking advantage of a position of power over another person.

ward of the state. Adult or child who is appointed a legal guardian to oversee his affairs.

writ of mandamus. Court order designed to compel a judicial or governmental officer to perform a duty owed to a petitioner.

Resources

This section is intended to provide readers with descriptions and contact information of organizations that deal with guardianship issues and concerns.

One of the most important elements of guardianship victim advocacy is providing effective education and resources to those being impacted by the guardianship industry. The feelings of despair, abandonment, and hopelessness so commonly associated with guardianships can be immobilizing. By compiling this list of pertinent organizations, I have attempted to dispel these sentiments. These resources are all available at no cost to individuals or family members trapped in guardianship proceedings or trying to prevent unnecessary guardianships.

Many of these organizations understand the damage that fraudulent guardianships can cause and in their own way are trying to create a better system. Whether in the form of a telephone call, an email, or a letter, reporting injustice in guardianships is our responsibility as good citizens. Even if you do not speak to someone directly, leave a message with your story. Do not leave it unsaid. A single well-written complaint may lead to a tipping point in awareness and change an entire probate system.

Whether your need is simply to be heard, to fight for better legislation, or to report wrongdoing in the court, this resource list will help you contact the appropriate agencies to do so.

The contact information of each organization is, of course, subject to change at any time.

ADVOCACY ORGANIZATIONS

Americans Against Abusive Probate Guardianship (AAAPG)
5630 Oaktree Ave.
Hollywood, FL 33312
Phone: (855) 913-5337
Website: www.aaapg.net
Email: info@aaapg.net
AAAPG is a national non-profit organization focusing attention on the plight of victims of guardianship abuse. Based in South Florida with affiliate organizations in multiple states, its goal is to educate, advocate, and legislate in support of meaningful guardianship reform.

The Al Katz Center for Holocaust Survivors & Jewish Learning, Inc.
5710 Cortez Road West
Bradenton, FL 34210
Phone: (941) 313-9239
Website: www.alkatzcenter.org
Email: helpelders@hotmail.com
The Al Katz Center is a not-for-profit corporation serving the needs of the elderly Jewish and non-Jewish communities. In addition to sponsoring many humanitarian programs and events, the center offers free support to elders in need or guardianship crises nationwide.

Catherine Falk Organization
Website: http://catherinefalkorganization.org
Email: catherine@catherinefalkorganization.org
This organization actively seeks legislation change across the United States to provide visitation rights to those denied access to a loved one. It has helped the passage of the Peter Falk Bill, commonly known as "right of association" legislation, in a number of states. This bill addresses isolation and visitation rights violations against wards and families by unscrupulous guardians. This organization also provides resources to individuals who are being denied access to family members.

Center for Guardianship Certification (CGC)

P.O. Box 5704

Harrisburg, PA 17110

Phone: (717) 238-4689

Website: www.guardianshipcert.org

Email: info@guardianshipcert.org

The Center for Guardianship Certification offers a comprehensive guardianship certification program to every professional guardian, in hopes of encouraging best practices and fostering excellence in the guardianship industry.

Coalition for Elder & Disability Rights (CEDAR)

Website: www.coalition4rights.com

CEDAR's focus is human rights of the elderly and disabled. It investigates elder abuse and human rights violations primarily in California. Its advocates are at the forefront of education, policy analysis, and research on these issues. It presents its findings at conferences and events across the nation.

Elderdignity.org

Website: http://elderdignity.org

Email: elderdignity@hotmail.com

This website was created as a result of an advocacy campaign for a woman who had been caught in the guardianship system. Today, its mission is to raise public awareness of systemic issues and abuses in state guardianship systems throughout the United States, to advocate for victims, and to be a voice for guardianship reform and elder dignity.

Families Against Court Embezzlement Unethical Standards (F.A.C.E.U.S.)

Website: http//faceus.org

Email: info@faceus.org

This organization's stated mission is to eliminate guardianship abuse in the United States. It advocates on behalf of our most vulnerable citizens, including the elderly, disabled, and veterans, and encourages the passage of new legislation to prevent new cases of abuse.

Guardianship Reform Advocates for the Disabled and Elderly (G.R.A.D.E.)

Phone: (210) 838-6493

Website: www.guardianshipreform.org

Email: khood490@aol.com

G.R.A.D.E.'s mission is to support guardianship reform at the state and federal levels. It advocates for victims and their families and strives to be a resource that can be used by fellow advocates in every state.

Kasem Cares

2372 Morse Ave., Suite 369

Irvine, CA 92614

Phone: (949) 872-0658

Website: www.kasemcares.org

Led by Kerri Kasem, this organization's mission is to eliminate all forms of elder abuse, including isolation, through education and awareness, as well as support of social change and legislative action.

National Association to Stop Guardianship Abuse (NASGA)

P.O. Box 886

Mt. Prospect, IL 60056

Website: https://stopguardianabuse.org

Email: info@guardianship.org

NASGA seeks to protect the rights of vulnerable individuals who have been described as "incompetent" and made wards of the state in unlawful and abusive guardianships or conservatorships. It wishes to reform state systems by amendment of existing statutes and increased penalties against violations of law.

National Disability Rights Network (NDRN)

820 1st St. NE, Suite 740

Washington, DC 20002

Phone: 202-408-9514

Website: www.ndrn.org

Email: info@ndrn.org

The National Disability Rights Network is a non-profit membership organization for the federally mandated Protection and Advocacy (P&A) Systems and Client Assistance Programs (CAP). There is a P&A/CAP agency in every state and territory in the country, as well as one serving the Native American population in the four corners region. Collectively, the P&A/CAP network is the largest provider of legally based advocacy services to people with disabilities in the United States. To find the NDRN member agency in your state, click on the map of the United States located on the homepage of the NDRN's website.

National Resource Center for Supported Decision-Making (NRC-SDM)

Phone: (202) 448-1448

Website: www.supporteddecisionmaking.org

Email: JHJP@dcqualitytrust.org

This organization seeks to demonstrate supported decision-making as a valid form of guardianship that should be considered before substituted decision-making. It helps bring together other groups that best represent the interests of older adults and people with intellectual and developmental disabilities. Its website provides detailed descriptions of the guardianship laws of each state.

Spectrum Institute

555 S. Sunrise Way, Suite 205

Palm Springs, CA 92264

Phone: (818) 230-5156

Website: http://spectruminstitute.org

Email: tomcoleman@spectruminstitute.org

This organization has two programs. The Disability and Abuse Project identifies ways to reduce the risk of abuse, promotes healing for victims, and seeks justice for those who have been victimized by physical, sexual, emotional, or financial abuse or exploitation. The Disability and Guardianship Project is designed to promote access to justice for adults with cognitive and communication disabilities who are involved in guardianship proceedings, and to promote viable alternatives to guardianship.

GOVERNMENTAL ORGANIZATIONS

Administration for Community Living (ACL)

330 C St. SW

Washington, DC 20201

Phone: (202) 401-4634

Website: www.acl.gov

Created by the U.S. Department of Health and Human Services, the Administration for Community Living seeks to maximize the independence, well-being, and health of older adults, people with disabilities across the lifespan, and their families and caregivers. The ACL awards grants to states and organizations, which then use this money to provide services and support to older adults and people with disabilities, conduct research, and develop innovative approaches to doing both. The ACL maintains eight regional offices throughout the United States, each covering a specific region of the country.

Elder Justice Initiative (EJI)

U.S. Department of Justice (DOJ)

950 Pennsylvania Ave. NW

Washington, DC 20530-0001

Phone for Eldercare Locator Helpline: (800) 677-1116

Phone for Victim Connect Hotline: (855) 484-2846

Website: www.justice.gov/elderjustice

Created by the U.S. Department of Justice, the mission of this program is to support and coordinate the DOJ's enforcement and programmatic efforts to combat elder abuse, neglect, and financial fraud and scams that target seniors in the United States. It provides targeted training and resources to elder justice professionals; investigates and prosecutes financial scams targeting older adults; promotes federal, state, and local coordination to resolve cases of grossly substandard elder care; and connects older adults and their families or caregivers with appropriate investigative agencies.

National Center on Elder Abuse (NCEA)

c/o University of Southern California Keck School of Medicine

Department of Family Medicine and Geriatrics

1000 South Fremont Ave., Unit 22, Building A-6

Alhambra, CA 91803

Phone: (855) 500-3537

Website: https://ncea.acl.gov

Email: ncea-info@aoa.hhs.gov

Run by the U.S. Administration on Aging (AoA), the National Center on Elder Abuse (NCEA) is a national resource center dedicated to the prevention of elder mistreatment. Although it does not investigate cases of elder abuse itself, the NCEA distributes information on the subject of elder abuse to professionals and the public, and provides technical assistance and training to states and community-based organizations.

National Center on Law & Elder Rights (NCLER)

Website: https://ncler.acl.gov

Email: NCLER@acl.hhs.gov

Created through a contract with the Administration on Community Living (ACL), which is part of the U.S. Department of Health and Human Services, the NCLER is designed to support and protect the rights, financial security, and independence of older adults. It is a resource center for legal services and aging and disability networks, focusing on the legal rights of older adults. It offers free case consultation assistance to attorneys and professionals seeking more information to help older adults. Unfortunately, its services are not available to the general public.

U.S. Government Accountability Office (GAO)

441 G St. NW

Washington, DC 20548

Phone: (202) 512-3000

Website: www.gao.gov

Email: contact@gao.gov

The U.S. Government Accountability Office (GAO) is an independent, non-partisan agency that works for Congress. Its stated mission is to support Congress in meeting its constitutional responsibilities and to help improve the performance and ensure the accountability of the federal government for the benefit of the American people.GAO investigates how the federal government spends taxpayer dollars. While its main focus is on federal practices and expenditures, it does have the ability to report on statewide elder abuse and has done so in the past.

United States Senate Special Committee on Aging

G31 Dirksen Senate Office Building

Washington, DC 20510

Phone: (202) 224-5364

Website: www.aging.senate.gov

Established in 1961, this committee is composed of thirteen senators, split along party lines. While the committee does not have any legislative authority, its purpose is to study issues related to older Americans, conduct oversight of programs for the elderly, and investigate reports of fraud targeting the elderly. In December 2007, the committee released a report entitled Guardianship for the Elderly: Protecting the Rights and Welfare of Seniors with Reduced Capacity. *While the report quotes its 2003 Chairman, Larry Craig, as saying, "Ironically, the imposition of guardianship without adequate protections and oversight may actually result in the loss of liberty and property for the very persons these arrangements are intended to protect," the committee has done little to follow up on what were obvious problems of guardianship even then.*

NON-GOVERNMENTAL ORGANIZATIONS

American Bar Association Commission on Law and Aging

Washington, DC Office

1050 Connecticut Ave. NW, Suite 400

Washington, DC 20036

Phone: (202) 662-1000

Website: www.americanbar.org/groups/law_aging/resources/ guardianship_law_practice.html

The American Bar Association Commission on Law and Aging deals with issues related to the legal rights, dignity, autonomy, quality of life, and quality of care of aging persons. The commission accomplishes its work through research, policy development, advocacy, education, training, and assistance to lawyers, bar associations, and other groups working on issues of aging. This committee's section of the ABA's website contains pages on guardianship law practice and elder abuse.

Center for Elders and the Courts (CEC)

National Center for State Courts

300 Newport Ave.

Williamsburg, VA 23185

Phone: (800) 616-6164

Website: www.eldersandcourts.org

The Center for Elders and the Courts (CEC) is a project within the National Center for State Courts. It serves as the primary resource for the judiciary and court management on issues related to aging, including adult guardianship. The center strives to increase judicial awareness of these issues; provide training tools and resources to improve court responses to elder abuse and adult guardianships; and develop a collaborative community of judges, court staff, and aging experts.

Center for Elder Rights Advocacy (CERA)

Website: https://legalhotlines.org

Email: info@ceraresource.org

Center for Elder Rights Advocacy is a project of Elder Law of Michigan, with a grant from the Administration on Aging. Its mission is to provide technical assistance to legal hotline managers, developers, and other stakeholders for non-profit legal programs that provide telephone legal advice. While its legalhotlines. org website was designed to provide information on setting up a non-profit legal hotline, CERA also provides a state-by-state listing of all available senior legal hotlines and other senior legal services. To access this information, use the map located on the website's landing page. Please note that some states do not have hotlines.

National Guardianship Association (NGA)

174 Crestview Drive

Bellefonte, PA 16823

Phone: (877) 326-5992

Website: www.guardianship.org

Email: info@guardianship.org
The National Guardianship Association is comprised of a diverse group of guardianship practitioners and allied professionals across the United States. It seeks to protect adults under guardianship by ensuring that their guardians receive quality education and access to resources. The association is recognized as the leading national resource for professional development.

Working Interdisciplinary Network of Guardianship Stakeholders (WINGS)
ABA Commission on Law and Aging
Washington, DC Office
1050 Connecticut Ave. NW, Suite 400
Washington, DC 20036
Phone: (202) 662-8693
Website: www.naela.org/NGN (Click on "WINGS" tab)
WINGS is made up of court-based professional and community groups and focused on identifying and advocating for legislative changes dealing with guardianships laws. This program is sponsored by the American Bar Association. It sets up national conferences, provides suggestions for law reform, and has established pilot WING programs in several states to carry out its missions.

GENERAL INFORMATION

The AARP Public Policy Institute (American Association of Retired Persons)
601 E St. NW
Washington, DC 20049
Phone: (202) 434-3840
Website: www.aarp.org/ppi
Email: ppi@aarp.org
Run by the AARP, this institute was formed in 1985 to promote the development of sound, creative policies to address the common need of older Americans for economic security, healthcare, and quality of life. In 2006, it released a report entitled Guardianship Monitoring: A National Survey of Court Practices, *which highlights a number of important issues within the guardianship system, including the need for increased guardian training and the general lack of accountability. This report does not, however, discuss the widespread abuse of elderly wards.*

American Civil Liberties Union (ACLU)

125 Broad St., 18th Floor

New York NY 10004

Phone: (212) 549-2500

Website: www.aclu.org (Click on the "Issues" tab and choose "Disability Rights" and then "Integration and Autonomy of People with Disabilities" from the drop-down menu.)

The ACLU is a non-partisan organization whose stated mission is "to defend and preserve the individual rights and liberties guaranteed to every person in this country by the Constitution and laws of the United States." Through its lobbying efforts and its practice of court litigation, it attempts to defend, clearly define, and strengthen the civil liberties of all people. As an organization, it is aware of the problems inherent in adult guardianship proceedings and encourages supported decision-making as an alternative approach to these issues.

Medical Certificate of Capacity

https://onedrive.live.com/view.aspx?resid=5DA8C19320796548!4174 &ithint=file%2cdocx&app=Word&authkey=!Alm159kFap_a95E

A Medical Certificate of Capacity establishes that an individual had full capacity on a particular date. It is designed to certify that any preneed documents created for your estate plan were properly executed by you as a fully capacitated individual. This may prevent claims that you were incapacitated at some unspecified time in the past and reduce the risk of the court attempting to void your preneed documents. The entire form should be witnessed and updated often. A downloadable version may be found at the link above.

National Center for State Courts (NCSC)

300 Newport Ave.

Williamsburg, VA 23185

Phone: (800) 616-6164

Website: www.ncsc.org

The National Center for State Courts is an independent, non-profit court organization designed to provide state trial and appellate courts and their administrative offices with authoritative knowledge and information. It does so by collaborating with the Conference of Chief Justices, the Conference of State Court Administrators, and other associations of judicial leaders. Its main goal is to ensure judicial administration that supports fair and impartial decision-making. It acts as a clearinghouse for research information and comparative data to achieve this goal.

National College of Probate Judges (NCPJ)

300 Newport Ave.

Williamsburg, VA 23185

Phone: (800) 616-6165

Website: www.ncpj.org

Email: ncpj@ncsc.org

The NCPJ is managed by the National Center for State Courts. It is the only national organization exclusively dedicated to improving probate law and probate courts, which generally handle cases involving the estates of deceased persons, adult guardianship and protective proceedings, and mental health and addictive disease treatment, and matters concerning developmentally disabled persons. The NCPJ's stated purpose is to promote efficient, fair, and just judicial administration in the probate courts, and to provide opportunities for continuing judicial education for probate judges and related personnel.

Uniform Law Commission (ULC)

111 N. Wabash Ave., Suite 1010

Chicago, IL 60602

Phone: (312) 450-6600

Website: www.uniformlaws.org

The Uniform Law Commission (also known as the National Conference of Commissioners on Uniform State Laws) was established in 1892 to provide states with non-partisan legislation that attempts to simplify and clarify critical areas of state statutory law such as probate law. While the ULC offers language for changes to existing guardianship laws in probate courts, state legislatures must first approve these suggested changes before they can be enacted. All ULC members must be lawyers, qualified to practice law.

FILMS / DOCUMENTARIES

Broken—The Fallout from Guardianship Abuse

www.youtube.com/watch?v=jUzjkc8Y0QM&t=62s

In this one-hour AAAPG-produced documentary, the organization's members and their families offer commentary on the state of guardianship in the United States as well as numerous firsthand stories of guardianship abuse.

Edith + Eddie

www.kartemquin.com/films/editheddie

This Oscar-nominated documentary short features Edith and Eddie, ages 96 and 95, who are America's oldest interracial newlyweds. Their unusual and heartwarming love story is disrupted by a family feud that threatens to tear the couple apart through the imposition of guardianship.

Guardianship at Probate Court

https://vimeo.com/146638349

Presented by magistrate Paula Haas of Summit County Probate Court, this video explains guardianship and its different types, how a person becomes a guardian, and what you need to know as you consider becoming a guardian.

The Guardians

www.guardiansdocumentary.com

This documentary film investigates allegations of corruption against the Nevada Guardianship and Family Court systems and shines a light on the lucrative business of guardianship, which drains seniors' life savings and takes away their rights.

Pursuit of Justice—A Film on Guardianship Reform

http://pursuitofjusticefilm.com

The documentary is intended to be used as an educational and advocacy tool to improve access to justice for seniors and people with various types of disabilities—disabilities that might bring them into contact with guardianship or conservatorship proceedings in state courts. It tracks the activities of a civil rights attorney, a clinical psychologist, and a small but growing network of supporters as they advocate for reform of state guardianship and conservatorship systems. These advocates expose systematic injustices that have been affecting hundreds of thousands of Americans of all ages.

WXYZ Detroit News

"Michigan families speak out about losing loved ones to guardianship"

https://www.wxyz.com/news/local-news/investigations/michigan-families-speak-out-about-losing-to-loved-ones-to-guardianship

This news segment by WXYZ's Heather Catallo focuses on the issue of losing loved ones to guardianship.

About the Author

Sam Judah Sugar, MD, was born in Norrkoping, Sweden, in 1947, the first son of Bergen Belsen concentration camp survivors Abe and Rosalie Sugar. The couple was miraculously found alive in a Red Cross-created displaced persons camp in Sweden by cousins from Illinois. With the help of the Hebrew Immigrant Aid Society, they immigrated to Chicago in 1949.

Dr. Sugar's primary school education was in the Chicago Jewish Day School movement. He attended high school at the Chicago Jewish (Ida Crown) Academy, where he lettered in basketball, was active in student government, and was elected vice president of his senior class. He received a BA in the social sciences from the University of Illinois, Chicago, and was honored as an Edmund J. James Scholar. In 1972, he was awarded an MD degree from the Abraham Lincoln College of Medicine at the University of Illinois, Chicago. From 1972 through 1975, he was a house officer at Evanston Hospital in Evanston, Illinois, his last year serving as chief resident in internal medicine. He achieved certification as a specialist in internal medicine from the American Board of Internal Medicine in 1976, and was distinguished as a fellow of the American College of Physicians in 1981.

After establishing a private practice, Dr. Sugar created the first managed care independent practice association and outpatient infusion center in his area. He then became physician director for managed care at Evanston/Northwestern Healthcare. Dr. Sugar has held faculty positions at Northwestern University Feinberg School of Medicine and the Chicago Medical School.

He was first exposed to guardianship in the case of a family member. What he saw in probate court was so alarming that it forced him to question how such a system of judicially endorsed constitutional violations possibly could exist in the United States. Through social media, Dr. Sugar began to connect with dozens of others who had experienced guardianship abuse all over the country.

After a chance meeting with Lidya Abramovici, another Florida probate victim, Dr. Sugar organized what would ultimately become the Americans Against Abusive Probate Guardianship, or AAAPG, in 2014, with "Educate, Advocate, Legislate" as its motto. Along with a small number of other Florida victims, they lobbied hard in Tallahassee, Florida, to change the state's guardianship statutes. Thanks to these lobbying efforts, in 2015 and 2016, the Florida legislature near unanimously passed significant legislative guardianship reforms.

AAAPG is a continuously growing national organization composed of victims and their families from nearly every state in the union. Through proprietary research, surveys, interviews, and testimonials, AAAPG has been able to construct a detailed picture of the guardianship industry and its abuses.

Dr. Sugar lives in Hollywood, Florida, with his wife, Judy. They have four children and eleven grandchildren.

Index

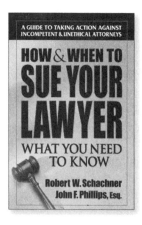